THE ART
O F
VANISHING

THE ART

OF

VANISHING

A MEMOIR OF
WANDERLUST

LAURA SMITH

VIKING

VIKING

An imprint of Penguin Random House LLC

375 Hudson Street

New York, New York 10014

penguin.com

Insert pages 1 (top, bottom); 2 (top, middle, bottom); 4 (top, bottom); 5 (top, bottom); 6 (top, bottom); and 8: Barbara Newhall Follett papers. Rare Book & Manuscript Library, Columbia University
in the City of New York, and ©Stefan Cooke/Farksolia.org

Insert page 3: Laura Smith

Insert page 7 (top): Arthur Griffin/The Life Picture Collection/
Getty Images

Insert page 7 (bottom): ©Stefan Cooke/Farksolia.org

ISBN: 9780399563584 (hardcover)
ISBN: 9780399563607 (e-book)

Printed in the United States of America
1   3   5   7   9   10   8   6   4   2

Set in Adobe Garamond Pro

Penguin is committed to publishing works of quality and integrity.
In that spirit, we are proud to offer this book to our readers;
however, the story, the experiences, and the words
are the author's alone.

For P.J.

THE ART

O F

VANISHING

ONE

I have long been in the habit of passing by houses and wondering about the people who live inside. I grew up in a residential neighborhood in Washington, D.C., the kind where the homes are close together and neighbors often wind up knowing more than they might like to. Before dinner, I would escape my house to walk our little white lapdog. The predictability of the ritual—setting the table, filling water glasses, the sight of my parents' briefcases in the hall—filled me with dread. A day had ended exactly as it had the day before, and it would end the exact same way the next day and possibly forever.

This wasn't how I wanted my life to be. I imagined that when I grew up, I would live all over the world. I would be an explorer of the wilderness, an observer of animals, a connoisseur of cultures, a collector of the unfamiliar. I envisioned hastily packed suitcases, maps, binoculars, huts in the mountains, spare hotel rooms in dusty cities, Jeeps tearing down muddy roads into the jungle.

As I wandered the streets of my neighborhood, I was shopping for other possibilities, other lives lived in other houses. But those lives appeared to be exactly the same as mine. In well-lit dining rooms and kitchens I saw other families setting the table, calling the children downstairs, washing their dishes in the sinks.

Television screens illuminated family rooms where exhausted parents slumped on couches after a long day in the office. Children did their homework by the glow of Pottery Barn desk lamps. I imagined that after their parents went to sleep, when the loneliness of those quiet hours became too much to bear, they whispered to each other beneath their sheets.

During the day they roamed the perimeters of their neighborhoods on bicycles and were driven to soccer and piano practice. They learned about faraway places in textbooks and on the news, but it seemed as if there had never been anything but this, no other place than here. Thirty years on they would come back to houses like these and do the same things all over again.

I wasn't sure what my mother did for a living, though I had memorized her job title because it sounded important and I was proud that it might be. "She's a health policy analyst," I told a friend. "What does that mean?" the friend asked. "It means she saves lives," I said, feeling fairly confident that this wasn't true, except perhaps in an abstract sense. But I wanted it to be true. I wanted the stakes of daily life to be more exciting than desks, screens, and fluorescent lights.

I passed by house after house, each one a nighttime domestic diorama: *Homo sapiens suburbae*. These people had nothing to do with the world of mystery, dark deeds, and wilderness that I was sure was out there somewhere. My house—if I had a house—would be different. It would be in the mountains, or the jungle, or maybe in the middle of a city. My children and I would eat ice cream before dinner and play freeze tag at night by the light of fireflies. We would have a menagerie of animals. If you stood outside our house at night, you would hear peals of laughter. You would see tickle wars and pillow fights in warm, glowing rooms. But then another thought struck me: what if the reason all these people lived the same lives was that this was the only way?

As I grew older, the fantasy began to erode. Where would the money come from? Would I have a partner, someone to help me? Where would the Jeep in the jungle take me and for what purpose? Where would my children go to school? Would I even have children?

When I was in my midtwenties, I heard a story about a young woman who had also dreamed of leading a life of adventure, and I could not get it out of my head. Her name was Barbara Newhall Follett. She was a child prodigy and had published an acclaimed novel at the age of twelve. People called her a genius. A photograph was taken as she corrected her proofs with a quill, smiling proudly at someone to the left of the photographer. When she was thirteen, she left her parents and traveled the high seas with a hardened crew. Later that year she published a memoir about the experience. She was deeply knowledgeable about botany, butterflies, and much of the natural world. She was an accomplished violinist and a talented poet, but above all she was a writer. She had been writing short stories since the age of five.

"She's your kind of person," my friend Robert said when he pointed me to an article about her. I had led an ordinary childhood and no one has ever accused me of being a genius, but Barbara and I shared a love of literature and the outdoors. There was something else too: a certain temperamental similarity—a restlessness. Later I began to wonder about Robert's true motivation for telling me about her. When she was almost exactly my age, she vanished without a trace. He knew I would want to find her.

It happened on December 7, 1939. The residents of Brookline, Massachusetts, were busily preparing for Christmas. Miss Ayers's shop on Beacon Street was selling Christmas wrapping paper, ribbons, and stationery. Hendries's offered ice cream sculpted in the shape of Santa Claus. The Village Flower Shop was stocked full of poinsettias, and all around town people were placing orders for turkeys at nineteen cents a pound. As night set in, the temperature hovered around freezing and the gas lamps flickered in the darkness. Families prepared for dinner in their clapboard houses on Walnut Street and their Victorian houses with trellised porches on Cyprus Street.

For some, the looming holidays brought a twinge of pain, their sadness cast in sharp relief against the holiday cheer. A fifteen-year-old boy ran away from school that day. A middle-aged woman didn't come home that night. Four people reported their dogs missing, and a twenty-two-year-old girl slit her wrists and then disappeared.

On Kent Street, Barbara's marriage was coming to an end. The young couple's apartment was comfortable but modest, with a fireplace and a rounded row of windows overlooking the quiet street below. She was twenty-five, fine featured and tomboyish, with a long auburn bob. She hadn't planned on this kind of life. She hadn't planned on bickering about who would hang the curtains or what music to play at a dinner party. She had never intended to sit in an office all day, a large round clock ticking the minutes away. She hadn't planned on having a husband or a house.

The Boston and Albany Railroad had a depot around the corner and Black Falcon station, with its enormous ships fastened in the harbors, was just five miles away. There were ways to escape from Brookline, to get out of a marriage, to alter the patterns of a life. Barbara gathered her notebook and thirty dollars. She walked out of the apartment, down the engraved wooden staircase, through the front door, and disappeared into the night. She was never seen or heard from again.

The apartment was exactly as I had envisioned it: in a low-rise building with rounded turrets and a plain façade in a quiet neighborhood of small apartments and clapboard houses, with a few shops and restaurants. A few houses down, an old man in a neatly pressed button-down shirt was mowing his lawn. Brookline is a town that seems to belong to another time, giving it a Halloween feel regardless of the season. There was a whiff of mystery, a sense that something more was going on behind those well-kept exteriors. Or maybe I was reading into it because I knew something had happened in that building seventy-five years before.

I was lurking in front of Barbara's building when a middle-aged Australian woman came out to put her trash in the dumpster. We started talking. I explained that this was the last place Barbara had been seen. "Would you like to come inside?" she asked.

A few moments later, I stood in front of the large, curved living-room windows, wondering if this very apartment had been Barbara's. Below the window, I could hear the man mowing his lawn. I wondered how many Saturdays, for how many years, he had done exactly that. The mechanical hum of the mower was oddly comforting. The woman's boxer, Harry, butted his snout against my legs while I answered her questions. I was looking for Barbara, I said. I doubted I would find her, but I hoped to gather clues and learn more. I had reason to believe that she was the vanishing type, capable of erasing one life and creating another. But there were other, more sinister possibilities to consider as well.

I was just a year older than Barbara when she vanished, and this fact seemed significant to me. I had a sense that the decisions I was making then would determine the rest of my life. Like with a rocket ship, the trajectory set on the ground was critical; a fraction of a degree in the wrong direction could send me to a wildly different place.

Somewhere along the line, in ways barely perceptible at first, things went wrong for Barbara. From my vantage point, her life was both an inspiration and a warning. But I couldn't think of how to explain this to the Australian woman, so I thanked her and left.

TWO

In 1926, Barbara sat at her typewriter in the second story of a wood-paneled cottage in New Haven, Connecticut. She had freckles, long brown ringlets, an intense gaze, and a puckish upturned nose. Her fingers moved rapidly as she typed. *Clackety-clack-clack-clack-clack* went the sound of the typewriter's iron keys as they landed on the paper, followed by the metal carriage sliding back. *Clack-clack-clack-clack-clack.* She had decorated the room herself and had chosen a wallpaper with gold and bronze birds and plants because she wanted to be surrounded by wild things. She was writing a novel about running away, and though she didn't know it yet, it would soon make her famous.

Barbara was born into a literary family. Her father, Wilson Follett, was an English professor at Dartmouth when she was born, and he became an editor at Yale University Press when she was five. He was a handsome man with a serious face, a sharp dresser who favored a Norfolk jacket and a bow tie. He took fastidious care of his clothes because he didn't have many. He had never been good with money. An excellent conversationalist, he'd graduated magna cum laude from Harvard and was said to have had a photographic memory. Women found him charming.

Barbara's mother, Helen Thomas Follett, was a writer and literary critic. She cowrote articles with Wilson that appeared in the *Atlantic Monthly* and the *Yale Review,* mostly about literature and composition. When Barbara was four, her parents published *Some Modern Novelists,* a collection of essays on various authors including Joseph Conrad, whose talents Wilson was early to recognize, and Henry James, whom the Folletts described as "a slender and shrinking youth of incredible unsophistication." But Barbara consumed much of Helen's time. Helen stayed home with her, and as Barbara grew up, Helen's writings shifted to focus primarily on her education. She wrote articles for parenting magazines and manuals on teaching children to type. Barbara had Helen's expressive brown eyes and a strong brow, which gave her a willful, coltish look. She wasn't shy about saying exactly what she thought, asked or not.

Barbara's parents were certain from the beginning that hers would be a remarkable story. They went to great lengths to record every detail. Like many parents, they kept a baby book, and if baby books can be measured on a spectrum of obsession, the Folletts' is toward the far end. It's a codiary written to Barbara that records all the minutiae of her achievements in the first four years of life, even her ability to bring a spoonful of water to her mouth. Her weight was measured and charted every week for her first year. From five to six in the evening, one-year-old Barbara had "organized play time" with both parents. The Folletts observed that she was "strong and determined" based on the way she hoisted herself up using the bars of her playpen.

Wilson wrote a three-page, single-spaced letter to a friend solely about Barbara's "baby mannerisms," which he entitled "Historia Barbarae." She was both specimen and beloved. It seems never to have occurred to him that his friend might not find Barbara's eating and sleeping habits quite so interesting as he did.

He even included a diagram of the rhythm at which she stamped her feet as he cooed "ti-tum, ti-tum, ti-tum."

Helen's entries in the baby book are just as doting. "Do you know how a mother's hands smooth out the cover over you, how tenderly, reverently? You will never know till some day the magic time comes for you, my Blessed, to be ever as I am now, a Mother." She wanted her words to be beautiful, her motherhood to be a work of art. The only pause in the baby book was a short period during World War I, when the Folletts worried that Wilson might be drafted.

Helen and Wilson were building a mythology around their baby. Though she was less than six months old, when she tried to roll over in her crib, they saw signs of the adventurer she would surely become. "Spiritually you were an explorer in unknown lands, a voyager in uncharted seas," Wilson wrote. This was just the beginning, "the first of your lives." Like a demigod with many incarnations, there would be other lives just as fabulous to come. "You are an ageless incarnation of spirit, the rarefied essence of Baby, a creature of dream and desire and we know that you could dissolve into a wish and become only a dream-that-was-too-beautiful."

Love this rapturous, a child this perfect, was otherworldly. To love this much was to be reminded of the possibility of enormous loss. Helen and Wilson considered that they might wake up one morning to find the nursery empty, all her playthings gone, a quiet, empty house. "You're so precious a thing," Wilson wrote, "one doesn't see how this world can hold you."

Adoration bordering on delusion is a staple of parenthood, but Barbara was turning out to be a remarkably precocious child. By eighteen months she knew all her letters and could count to ten. At just under two years, she became fixated on a paper leaflet entitled "A Grammar for Thinkers." She would bring the leaflet to her mother and point to the punctuation.

"What is that?" she asked.

"A comma," Helen replied. She pulled out a piece of paper and drew commas and periods on it. "More commas!" Barbara cried, and Helen drew more. Language and letters delighted her. When she was three, the Folletts walked around the sleepy neighborhood in Hanover, New Hampshire, where they lived. Barbara would point to the gables of houses and say they were *A*s. The football field goals were *H*s. A door at an angle also made an A. Sometimes she saw letters that weren't there, their shapes cast on the ceiling by lamplight, creating visions only she could see. By three and a half, she could count to one hundred and do rudimentary addition and subtraction.

Wilson later reported that she had been typing ever since she was three. One day, he said, she approached him at his typewriter and pointed to the machine saying, "Tell me a story about it." Half an hour later, she had learned how to load the paper and use the keys. By the next day, she had composed her first written words: "Dear Cousin Helen: I love the red bird very much, and I thank you for it."

Barbara was a tomboy and Wilson and Helen encouraged her outdoor adventures and rough play. This was the Roaring Twenties and women had recently won the right to vote. Conservative ideas about gender loosened a little and some of this trickled into child-rearing. Sixteen years before Barbara was born, Charlotte Perkins Gilman praised the health benefits of being a tomboy. Joseph Lee, the father of the playground movement, argued in his book *Play in Education,* published the year after Barbara was born, that "tomboydom" aided in girls' emotional development and resulted in lifelong levelheadedness. "A girl should be a tomboy during the tomboy age, and the more of a tomboy she is, the better." Of course, he argued, the tomboy period should end. He suggested thirteen as a good age to make one's foray into femininity. Barbara regularly wore pants ten years before Katharine Hepburn was photographed in them, lifting eyebrows with what some called her "rebel chic" look.

As Barbara grew, her parents filled her world with animals and wilderness exploration. In the winter she followed her father in a sled as he skied. In the summer she chased butterflies through the potato patch near their house. She caught them with a net and put them in a sieve so she could record their markings. Then she released them back into the wild. She loathed the way lepidopterists classified butterflies by pinning them with a needle. In fact, she hated the idea of killing anything. "How one can look at the fuzzy yellow ball of a little chicken and then want to kill it is more than I can see," she wrote when she was nine years old. In another letter she wrote, "A few days ago, I again climbed Mill Rock . . . It made my heart sick to hear the sounds of hammering and an ax, for I knew they were building up those wonderful forests."

In the summer, the Folletts rented a cabin on Lake Sunapee in New Hampshire. Barbara and her father would canoe along the shoreline, where the land came out like fingers into the water. There were lighthouses and endless trails through oak and pine forests. White-tailed deer roamed the woods, as did porcupines, moose, black bears, red foxes, and muskrats. Wild loons yodeled and arrived in great masses to feed on the golden trout and perch that lived in the pristine lake, which drew from cold underwater springs rising from a bedrock aquifer.

Barbara fed minnows on the lake's sandbars. She tried to count them, but with so many of them all flitting around each other it was as if they were one scintillating body. She put mussel shells in a box and hid them in a secret cave. She learned to dive and swim doggy paddle. "Open your eyes," Wilson cajoled her as she swam. There was a whole world of creatures down there, and he didn't want her to miss it. He built a wooden box with mesh wire nailed to the top for the salamanders she collected along the lake's mossy banks. The creatures' lethargic gait delighted her—the way they slowly lifted a limp back foot and placed it near the front foot before moving forward. She would let them walk on her hand, only to surprise them by placing another hand in front after they had completed the arduous journey across the first.

Barbara's mother took care of all the small details of daily life, but her father was the one who fascinated and delighted. He was her adventure companion. When she went hiking with him and his friend, they let her decorate their heads with flowers. She created charms and spells, and when she announced to her father that she had turned him into a kangaroo, he obligingly hopped around. When she tried to cast the spell on her mother, it didn't work.

When she was seven, she wrote a play about fairies and goblins that was likely inspired by the works of George MacDonald, the Scottish fantasy writer, whose books she devoured. Simultaneously, she was creating compendiums of imaginary birds, fish, and fairies with precise descriptions of the creatures' bodies, and habits. The Daylight Fuzzywing's "upper side is mostly white, but there is a band of orange around the wings with a row of six silver spots set in the band like precious stones, six of them on the upper wing, and four on the lower one." A friend of her parents drew pictures to match her descriptions of the imaginary butterflies.

She wrote stories about a planet called Farksolia, ruled by two children. The inhabitants lived in cities and left the wilderness untouched. She created the Farksolian census of hair color. The planet contained 40 Farksolians with black hair, 145 with auburn, and 500 blondes. She described the constellations that could be seen in the Farksolian sky and their complicated royal lineage.

She created an alphabet and language called Farksoo and wrote elaborate poems in Farksoo, all paeans to nature. "There are three tenses only: past present and future," she wrote. "The past is formed by suffixing vo to the root and pronoun: aravo, arovo, arivo etc." There were three ways to express the interrogative. Meaning changed depending on voice inflection. The sentence "Do you know whether or not you shall come" became "Laitro feer merlovai."

Wilson ordered two card-catalogue drawers from Boston so that Barbara could arrange the English-to-Farksoo dictionary in one and the Farksoo-to-English dictionary in the other. Barbara hoped that her friends from Farksolia would come in a boat and take her with them back to their perfect blue planet. "And if I ever come back, which would be doubtful," Barbara wrote, "I would never be contented with the Earth again."

Even at ten, she was self-aware enough to know that each

adventure made the ones that came before it seem ordinary; each path she cut through the woods made her crave the discovery of other paths. She was reading Robert F. Griggs's *The Valley of Ten Thousand Smokes,* about the discovery of the Katmai volcano in Alaska, and was captivated by the idea of exploration. When a friend wrote to say he had discovered a pond, she wrote back, "And to think of discovering it! The thrill of discovering a thing which no one else has ever seen!" She believed that satisfaction could be found in a place—it was just a matter of getting there.

Barbara's world was full of people, but few of them were children. Writers, publishers, and academics came and went, staying for dinner or longer. Barbara charmed a classics professor from the University of Wisconsin and exchanged letters with a close friend of Walt Whitman's. But her two greatest correspondents were Mr. Oberg, a Swedish émigré who ran an antique restoration shop in Providence, and Mr. St. John, a naturalist and dean of a theological seminary in New York. It was Mr. St. John who wrote to Barbara about discovering the pond, and she wrote back telling him everything she was reading, exploring, and thinking. She often referred to Mr. St. John as her "best friend" and "best traveling companion," enumerating the many adventures they would have together at Lake Sunapee. Mr. Oberg and Mr. St. John showered Barbara with gifts—furniture, moth cocoons, clocks, and stuffed animals—and she wrote back exuberantly: "Mr. St. John, I am crazy about the cocoons you sent me, and I, in spite of the fact that you told me a lot about them, have quite a lot to ask you." The decades between them didn't seem to bother her. Barbara's imaginary friends were adults as well: Beethoven, Wagner, and the Strausses. Once Wilson unknowingly nearly sat on one of her invisible friends at the breakfast table, but Barbara grabbed the chair, squealing, "Hey, that's Wagner's chair!"

The Folletts decided to homeschool her because they felt a girl of her precocious talents should not be in a traditional school. Helen explained in an essay in *Good Housekeeping* that ordinary schooling robs children of their uniqueness and gives them "a bored tolerance of the world." The Folletts made sure that Barbara was never bored. In her essay, Helen repeatedly referred to Barbara's schooling as "our adventure." "There has been only excitement in the discovery that the world was her special nut to crack," she wrote. "Asking questions, demanding answers, asking more questions for more answers became the formula in the house." Wilson would later write that he and Helen let Barbara "run wild, form associations by accident, and be mainly taught by experience and necessity . . . Nothing has as yet standardized her, or ironed out her spontaneity, or made her particularly ashamed of it. She has been given plenty of time to know herself."

It was a progressive time in education in the United States. The psychologist and educational reformer John Dewey wanted to abandon the tradition of rote memorization in favor of something more engaging. Much of what Helen and Wilson wrote about Barbara's education, especially regarding what Wilson described as "fostering a child's sense of natural order and beauty," recalls Maria Montessori's conception of "student-led learning." Montessori schools had begun to spread rapidly in the United States a few years before Barbara was born, but Wilson and Helen didn't see their method of education as following any established system. When Barbara was six, Wilson wrote that her education was "an experiment." They saw themselves as the master craftsmen of the most enchanted childhood.

Barbara was not free to run around in the woods all day. Quite the contrary: she was receiving a far more rigorous education than most children her age. When she was ten, a typical morning's lesson plan might include an hour on the piano, some violin, French verb conjugation, vocabulary practice, poetry memorization, and an oral exercise followed by arithmetic. "I am anxious to get through this commission business and get into interest with you—banking, etc.," Helen wrote in her instructions for Barbara when she was nine. Writing letters to her various adult correspondents was often part of the lesson plan, as was reading everything from *National Geographic* to Keats's poetry.

Stories about the wild consumed her—especially one. She was writing a novel about a little girl named Eepersip who ran away to the wilderness and vanished forever. Her pace was feverish: twelve hundred words an hour, four thousand to five thousand words a day. She could see it all so clearly; the lush dewy forest, the deer with their tails alert, the way that a lily seemed to pause just before it bloomed, overwhelmed by what it would become. "I wanted to run away," Barbara wrote later, "but, realizing the impossibility of it, I made someone else do it for me."

Barbara put a long note on her bedroom door outlining the conditions for entry:

Nobody may come into this room if the door is shut tight (if it is shut not quite latched it is all right) without knocking . . . If the door is shut tight and a person is in the room the shut door means that the person in the room wishes to be left alone.

She called her story *The House Without Windows*. In it, Eepersip is bored. One day, she wanders off, going deeper and deeper into the woods. She takes off her dress, replacing it with a dress of ferns. She weaves flowers into her hair and follows a new calendar, measured by years of wildness: "on the second day of her wildness"; "the first years of wildness . . ." It is a new life, "the wild life," and Eepersip has no intention of returning home—ever.

Though there are nymphs and fairies in the woods, Barbara wanted the setting of her novel to seem like a real place. As she worked through drafts over the course of her tenth and eleventh years, she tried to keep the flora and fauna consistent with the latitude, altitude, and season. There were blue and gold irises and "lady-slippers" in spring, and bright red cordary berries in winter. She left footnotes in the text that seem more like a botanist's log than anything from a child's fairy tale: "The cordary berry grows during the winter and is at its best by New Year"; "[the juice] keeps the kernel moist." She was drawing from her knowledge of New Hampshire, where she was born, Vermont and Maine, where she visited, and the woods near her house on Armory Street in New Haven. East Rock Park, with the Mill River running through it, was a short walk away, and just beyond that were the Quinnipiac River marshlands. She knew the woods in the book needed to be as vibrant as those places, perhaps suspecting that a fantasy's potency depends on the possibility it could happen. *What if?*

As she was putting the finishing touches on *The House*

Without Windows, she wrote of her yearning for a wilder life: "I want as long as possible in that green, fairylike, woodsy, animal-filled, watery, luxuriant, butterfly-painted, moth-dotted, dragonfly-blotched, bird-filled, salamandrous, mossy, ferny, sunshiny, moonshiny, long-dayful, short-nightful land, on that fishy, froggy, tadpoly, shelly, lizard-filled lake—[oh,] no end of the lovely things to say about that place, and I am mad to get there." Barbara is the girl inside the house, rattling at her cage, demanding to be set free. Go outside, she is saying. Embrace the world in all its frightening, joyful, sun-filled complexity.

The House Without Windows is a somewhat disturbing read. For one thing, Eepersip doesn't seem to care about her parents at all. She is never homesick, and the whole first third of the book is concerned with Mr. and Mrs. Eigleen's attempts to catch her, to grab an ankle or a shoulder, the end of her dress, but she is "light as a feather and graceful as a fern," and each time, she wriggles free.

Her parents suffer terribly. Mrs. Eigleen develops a nervous disorder: "She spent the spring in continual weeping and hysterics. Towards the summer she began to feel seriously ill." After Mr. Eigleen chases Eepersip up a tree, Barbara writes, "At last, in despair, he descended; and the people went away, leaving Eepersip in peace. . . . 'My, that was a dreary adventure!' she said sleepily, as she crawled off to find a place to sleep."

The heartsick parents are a nuisance. Eepersip sees their suffering but doesn't care. She makes several animal friends but abandons them quickly when a better adventure arises. She has no regrets. She misses no one. At another point, she discovers she has a little sister and returns home to peer into her bedroom window. She is enamored with the little girl and convinces her to run away and live the wild life with her. But unlike Eepersip, the little sister, Fleuriss, gets homesick. Eepersip is forced to bring her back.

As the two sisters say good-bye forever, Fleuriss asks, "Why don't you come home?—you've been away so long—and Mother cries for you still. Please come." Eepersip responds, "Oh, Fleuriss, I couldn't. If I were to go back home now, I should just die—even with you." After they part, "Eepersip stood on her tiptoes an instant: then, quick as a flash, she whirled about and bounded off, free—relieved of a gigantic burden."

In July of 1923, when Barbara was ten, Helen gave birth to another daughter, Sabra Wyman Follett, who was likely the inspiration for Fleuriss. Before the birth, Barbara's parents sent her to spend the summer in Sunapee with family friends, while they remained in New Haven. Barbara wrote letters to them every day, eagerly awaiting news of her sister's arrival. When Sabra was born, Barbara was delighted, announcing the birth to her friends in her letters: "Best of all I now have a little BABY SISTER." When Barbara finally came home in October, she was enchanted by Sabra, calling her "my little baby," and adding, "She is a little apple-blossom." Barbara watched Sabra as she gurgled and cooed, imagining that she desperately wanted to speak. As Sabra got older, Barbara wrote long exuberant descriptions of her attempts to crawl, sit up, and roll over. On pleasant days, Barbara wrote that they set the baby in the backyard for hours on end to enjoy the "fresh, woodsy air," noting how much her eyes shone afterwards.

The next summer, the Folletts brought Sabra to Sunapee, and Barbara reported that her sister loved the place as much as she did. When the family returned to New Haven, Barbara remarked, "I feel sure she misses being turned loose in the sand." When Sabra was two, the sisters began venturing into the woods together to collect pussy willows and moss. Barbara was nearly delirious with excitement to have an adventure companion. "She is *such* a delicious darling; such a rogue; so mischievous; so funny; so pretty; and so little." What Barbara did, Sabra mimicked. When Barbara touched moss, Sabra touched it. As Barbara typed letters to Mr. Oberg in her study, Sabra sat nearby perched on the couch watching her. She told Barbara she wanted to write letters to "Missha Oberg" too. Barbara wrote, "If I should try to describe her to you, it would be wasted energy, for she is too beautiful to be described." Yet she was unable to resist trying. She wrote about Sabra in almost every letter during those first few years of her life. In addition to Barbara's many ongoing writing projects, she was working on "an account of Sabra." She dedicated *The House Without Windows* to her.

In *The House Without Windows,* the scenes with the little sister are the only ones that hint at ambivalence, the only moments when the reader sees Eepersip loving someone. But still she leaves. In the end, Eepersip gets what she wants: she vanishes into thin air. As she stands deep in the forest, butterflies surround her and land on her wrists:

And then—she rose into the air, and, hovering an instant over a great laurel-bush, vanished. She was a fairy—a woodnymph. She would be invisible for ever to all mortals, save those few who have minds to believe, eyes to see. To these she is ever present, the spirit of Nature—a sprite of the meadow, a naiad of lakes, a nymph of the woods.

When Barbara finished the first draft of her novel, she handed it to her father. He reported studying the pages with the same editorial seriousness he would give to the books he was publishing. Though he didn't show it right away, he was delighted. "So much I found in it of the mighty swimmer, the enjoyable young comrade of trail and river, always ready to swing a paddle tirelessly or carry ungrumbling a full fair share of pack," he wrote. Barbara planned to give the novel to her mother. Would she like it? Yes, Wilson said. She certainly would. He had an idea. What if they tried to publish it? Barbara said she would like that very much.

The editing process was grueling. Barbara typed out passages and then crossed out words, phrases, and entire paragraphs with pencil. Penciled sentences hovered above scratched-out printed lines, and she scratched out even those and wrote them again. She wrote on the back when the page was too full. She cut pages in half with scissors and kept them piled up. She retyped passages and glued them over the passages she didn't like. Every page was covered in marks. No word went unscrutinized.

Since Wilson was working at Knopf, when Barbara was finished he brought the novel to them. She waited anxiously for the response, checking the mail every day. One day a letter arrived. It was blue, with Knopf's bounding borzoi logo stamped on the back. Her hands trembled as she held it. "I simply threw myself down on the floor and screamed, either with fear for what it might contain, with joy for getting it at last. . . . There is a feeling that, when it finally comes, it must be impossible—a dream—an optical illusion—a cross between those three things." Barbara tore open the letter and read. She let out a shriek of delight. "It is *Eepersip, The House Without Windows,* my *story,* my story in New York, with the Knopfs, to be *published*!! . . . PUBLISHED!!!!!!!"

The House Without Windows was published in 1926, when Barbara was twelve. Ernest Hemingway's *The Sun Also Rises* was published that same year. A year before, the *New Yorker* ran its first issue and F. Scott Fitzgerald's *The Great Gatsby* had come out. Willa Cather, Theodore Dreiser, and William Faulkner were publishing in that period as well. It's a wonder that a twelve-year-old's book was noticed at all, but *The House Without Windows* sold out before a single book was on the store shelves, and a second printing had to be ordered. The wunderkind darling of the Follett household became the wunderkind darling of the New York literary scene. H. L. Mencken, the tastemaking literary critic who founded the influential literary magazine *American Mercury,* praised the book. Blanche Knopf, the publisher responsible for the U.S. publication of Sigmund Freud, Simone de Beauvoir, and Albert Camus, sent Barbara a letter of congratulations. "Barbara is a genius," read the *Knickerbocker Press Magazine.* The *Daily Herald* called the book "a miracle."

Reviewers and readers loved Barbara precisely because she was young. She was a pure conduit to childhood, unfettered by adult thinking. Her verbal precocity enabled her to speak the language of adults, but from another, long-forgotten world. A reviewer in the *New York Times* wrote, "There can be few who have not at one time or another coveted the secret, innocent and wild at the same time, of a child's heart. And here is little Miss Barbara Follett, holding the long-defended gate wide open and letting us enter and roam at our will over enchanted ground." A reviewer at the *Saturday Review of Literature* suggested something similar: "This book grows almost unbearably beautiful. It becomes an ache in [one's] throat." Barbara's book was a reminder of all that was beautiful about childhood—and all that adults had lost.

With all of the positive reviews came one note of warning: "I can conceive of no greater handicap for the writer between the ages of nineteen and thirty-nine than to have published a successful book between the ages of nine and twelve." The reviewer, Anne Carroll Moore, argued in the *New York Herald Tribune* that the publishing world was too corrupt for the innocence of children, whose sensibilities are "unduly excited or prematurely deadened by such experience." Children had a right just to be children, unencumbered by questions of money and critical success. She had harsh words for the Follett parents about their methods of education: they had isolated her, robbed her of "variety of social relationships." Barbara needed "the companionship of other children." To Wilson, she wrote that rather than allowing Barbara to flourish free of the "Tyranny of Things," as he claimed he was doing in his conclusion to her book, he had opened its door and shoved her through. He had commoditized her. Moore warned, "What price will Barbara Follett have to pay for her 'big days' at the typewriter?"

Barbara fired back an angry two-page response: "I am very much amused at the favorable reviews which are being written—I do not take them at all seriously—but I do take seriously an article which distorts into a miserable caricature my living, my education, my whole personality." The message is clear: this was her story. She was the one making predictions.

Novels are one of the few places where authors can control the narrative entirely. Yet it's not clear that Barbara controlled even that. In 1925, she wrote to Mr. Oberg, "Daddy and I have been correcting it, to make it as perfect as we can." Wilson described his editorial process this way: "Barbara has been given by her parents, in the final preparation of this manuscript, exactly what help she has asked for. That is not nearly so much help as many an adult author often has from us, for there is not one idea or structural change of ours in the entire story. But I see no value in withholding solicited advice in order to make a Roman holiday for those who like to chuckle or guffaw over infantile slips in spelling and grammar. . . . When she wants to know: 'Have I made it clear what this means?' or 'Have I used this word twice too near together?' of course we say how it strikes us."

Barbara's drafts were covered in neat black script—handwriting that was not Barbara's, but Wilson's. Those edits go beyond correcting "infantile slips in spelling and grammar," though most are not major changes. Sentences are trimmed and reordered, repetitions removed. Occasionally parts of sentences are entirely scratched out and rewritten.

Barbara's "But when she got to the bottom she had seen houses; and so walking back or rather running as fast as she could, she decided that that wasn't the side for her," became, with Wilson's edits, "But when she got part way to the bottom she began to see houses; and so, deciding that that wasn't the side for her, she ran back."

He was smoothing the text, making it more fluid. Of course he's correct to point out that many adults' writing gets the same treatment by an editor. Barbara's letters are fluent and precocious. Her vocabulary rivals that of many adults. But writing a novel requires balancing specific details and ideas with a larger, sustained narrative arc. As anyone who is experienced with children knows, they think less linearly than novel writing typically requires. They are prone to spastic fits of inspiration and sometimes entirely nonsensical narrative turns. The uninhibited stream of consciousness of their storytelling is what is so charming about it. Some of this jubilance can be found in *The House Without Windows*. But it is tidy enough to make a reasonable reader wonder: Was this *really* just her work?

In Barbara's first draft, the book ends differently. Eepersip is reunited with two sisters (the second sister would later be edited out). Butterflies land on their foreheads and they are transformed into fairies, who stay in the woods forever. Barbara ends the book, "And please learn to love and respect <u>NATURE</u>. For if you do, she will love you, and you will be much happier. If you ever do hurt <u>NATURE</u> just remember that she will not do you any good turns. If you don't hurt <u>NATURE</u>, remember that she will do you a good turn. Remember how <u>NATURE</u> reunited the three loving sisters as a reward for their kindness to <u>HER</u>."

These lines are scratched out in wavering pencil lines (probably Barbara's), leaving the presumed last line of the book, "And when you catch a butterfly in your hat, be sure not to hurt it. . . . Remember, too, that that butterfly might be a fairy changing itself into a butterfly so you can see it."

That sounds like a child's writing. A second look at the published version reveals the intellectual and stylistic disparity between the two versions:

> She was a fairy—a wood-nymph. She would be invisible for ever to all mortals, save those few who have minds to believe, eyes to see. To these she is ever present, the spirit of Nature—a sprite of the meadow, a naiad of lakes, a nymph of the woods.

The syntax is much more complex—perhaps too complex for a child to have written. It's also a much more compelling ending. The reader does not get the satisfaction of seeing where Eepersip goes, the place where she finds lasting fulfillment. Barbara had been obsessed with pinning down exactly what the world looks like, what berries, what foliage, what birds and animals live there, but to spell out exactly how Eepersip had found satisfaction would have disappointed: nothing specific could be as tantalizing as the *idea* of satisfaction. The writer of those words knew that.

So who wrote them?

The ending recalls the entry Wilson had made in his diary when Barbara was a baby: "You are an ageless incarnation of spirit, the rarefied essence of Baby, a creature of dream and desire and we know that you could dissolve into a wish and become only a dream-that-was-too-beautiful." Wilson had been dreaming up a vanishing story ever since Barbara was born.

There is another possibility for how this ending came to be. It is possible that as Wilson sat at his desk, surrounded by his daughter's drafts, he was suddenly struck by an idea. What if Eepersip didn't just go off and live in the woods—what if she vanished off the face of the earth entirely? He wouldn't have to write the words himself exactly, just plant the idea, and then edit the language for fluidity.

There was much at stake. Not just Wilson's own vanity—to be the parent of a remarkable child is to be remarkable yourself—but also Barbara's dreams. She was young, her ego just forming, and failure at that age is devastating. There are ways you can nudge your child without realizing you're doing so, to protect without fully meaning to. Who wrote the end of *The House Without Windows* is not just a literary curiosity. It matters because that scene so closely mirrors what would happen to Barbara just over a decade later.

THREE

Around the time I started looking for Barbara, I decided to get married. I was ambivalent about marriage, but not about P.J. We'd been friends for three years in college before we started to date. My roommates had told me that he was interested in more than friendship, but I'd ignored them because I was dating someone else. On weekends he would pick me up in his Mercury Cougar to go grocery shopping, catch a movie, or eat sushi at the university cafeteria. During my senior year, I broke up with the boyfriend. When I told P.J. about the breakup at a crowded bar one night, I remember being struck by his reaction. He told me that it was my ex's loss. But there was something about his expression, and the tone of voice. He had just started dating someone else, and he sounded regretful. I considered him differently for a moment. What *would* it be like to date him? But our timing was off and I dismissed the idea.

P.J. broke up with his new girlfriend not long after. Then one night in my apartment, as we were watching a movie for film class, he leaned across the couch and kissed me. *Why not?* I thought. I hadn't been single in years and had missed out on the "hook-up culture" of college entirely. What my friends described was mostly unappealing—their experiences seemed to vacillate between slapstick comedy and disappointment, but I wanted to know what all the fuss was about.

One afternoon, a couple of weeks after the movie night, I was in a strip mall parking lot headed off to lunch with a friend when, as I slammed the car door, I was struck by a desperate desire to see P.J. as soon as possible. What was he doing at that exact moment and how quickly could I get this lunch over with?

Suddenly, he was transformed. He became strikingly handsome, with his elegant dark eyelashes and angular features. He had gripped me entirely, lodging an enormous steel fishing hook in my center. My long-held ideas about how to live suddenly mattered very little. *Oh,* I thought. *This is why people do what they do. This is why people buy houses together and have children. This is why they garden on the weekends.* Suddenly I saw all those things not as tedious burdens, but as monuments to love.

He had invited me to join him at a party that night. I called him on his cell phone when I arrived so that he would come outside. I wanted to see him for a moment alone. He had sensed my hesitance about the relationship and I wanted to reassure him. When he came out, his face was ashen. I realized he thought I had called him down to break up with him. "I'm into this," I said, and he looked thrilled.

"Want to sleep in the same place tonight?" he asked with a little too much excitement.

"Yes," I said.

We hadn't told our friends we were dating, partially because we didn't feel like having them make a fuss. That night, as we stood around talking, he secretly gripped my hand for a moment and I felt a rush.

On Valentine's Day, when we hadn't made clear plans (we'd been dating for only a few weeks at this point), I moped melodramatically through the day. I tried to go for a run but couldn't, and I got back into bed on the verge of tears at three in the afternoon. What had I become? How had the power shifted so suddenly? My phone rang and it was P.J. He asked me if I wanted to go get a beer. I decided I would break up with him because I couldn't stand the emotional turbulence of feeling this powerless anymore. I got into his car and told him I wanted to end it. He looked crestfallen and told me he felt the opposite, that he wanted us to date each other exclusively. He was so upset that he pulled over into a bank parking lot. The sun was setting and the colors were so dramatic that it nearly hurt to look at it. I said fine, knowing full well that this was what I had hoped he would say.

Life with P.J. was easy. We usually wanted to do the same things, which came as a huge relief. My previous relationship had been a constant battle over how to spend our time. My ex-boyfriend had mostly wanted to listen to lethargic jam bands stoned out of his mind. I wanted to hike, read, write, or go out with friends. A simple trip to the grocery store could cause an epic fight because we couldn't agree on how we would get there, when we would go, or even what we would buy. But moving through the day with P.J. was effortless.

Four years later, on the roof of our apartment in Washington, D.C., P.J. asked me to marry him. He was nervous and had turned around to face me too suddenly, which startled me. Yes, I said. Obviously yes.

It was other people who floated through their lives without

scrutiny. They were the ones who made a series of uninspired compromises that led them to lives of drudgery. I told myself I would never do that. But when people asked me why I had chosen to get married, I had no answer. I don't know, I said. Because sometimes people fall in love and want to announce to themselves and the world that they plan to stay together forever. Love was the factor I hadn't considered.

I didn't do a cost and benefit analysis. In fact, I hadn't thought much about marriage at all because marrying P.J. hadn't felt like a choice. He was a fact of life now. Questioning his place in it seemed as worthwhile as pondering whether I should keep my arms and legs. But I was squeamish about the wedding and skeptical of its meticulous choreography.

In Sartre's *Being and Nothingness* there is a section on "bad faith"—behaving without sincerity, lying to oneself. Sartre describes a café scene in which a waiter is serving his customers: "His movement is quick and forward, a little too precise, a little too rapid. He comes toward the patrons with a step a little too quick. He bends forward a little too eagerly . . . he is playing at being a waiter in a café." The waiter, as Sartre describes him, is imprisoned in his performance, relegating himself to the singular role that society allows him, rather than allowing himself the freedom of a more honest manner of being. What troubled me most about the concept of bad faith was not that we might lie to others, but that we might lie to ourselves. Self-deception is degrading. You wish you could have just a smidge more integrity. Your falseness lingers in the air and follows you through the day.

In the carefully scripted wedding rituals, I detected bad faith. I felt less like a bride and more like a person pretending to be a bride, the way a little girl might process through her living room with a pillowcase draped over her head toward some imaginary groom. I refused to take engagement photos because who would ever believe that we were spontaneously bounding through a field at sunset holding hands? Or making out in front of a brick wall? Who was this photo for? It couldn't be for us because anytime we looked at it we would know all the work that went into it: a long afternoon spent smiling to the point of jaw exhaustion.

I sidestepped this icky feeling by outsourcing the wedding planning to my mother. I announced to everyone that I could not be bothered to care about napkin colors or floral arrangements. The only things P.J. and I would deign to opine on were the things that truly mattered: the beer selection, the music, and the wedding cake, which would not be wedding cake because wedding cake tastes bad. We would eat pie. We also cared about the wedding ceremony, which we designed ourselves. These things—the food, the drinks, the music, the ceremony—turned out to be most of the details of the wedding.

The problem was that I both wanted to avoid dealing with the particulars of the wedding and that I came to see each choice as symbolic of the kind of life we would live together. As my mother went about happily making her plans, if they veered toward the traditional or the frilly I would swiftly intervene, outraged.

One night, P.J. and I went to my parents' house for dinner. We arrived with a pizza box in hand. I had decided that I wanted the wedding to be a pizza party (never mind that my father is gluten intolerant) held at the neighborhood bar, which was also a Ping-Pong hall. P.J. and my father sat silently at their ends of the table, looking wan, while my mother and I shouted viciously at each other. It was the kind of shouting that makes the neighbors wonder if they should call to see if everything is all right. My mother informed me in no uncertain terms that the family from Arkansas would not be coming all the way to D.C. for a pizza party at a Ping-Pong bar. She would have been more likely to agree to a wedding conducted on the moon in the nude. I informed her that, in that case, the family in Arkansas could attend a wedding at which the bride would not be present.

A few weeks later, my sister, my mother, P.J.'s mother, sister, and sister-in-law, and three of my friends gathered in a boutique for what was to be a long day of wedding dress shopping. The attention made me uncomfortable. I worried that they didn't really want to be there. Why would anyone want to follow someone around all day while they shopped for a dress? I tried on the first dress and announced, "This is it. I want to buy this one."

"What?" said the confused saleswoman. My friends and family (three of whom had traveled more than a hundred miles to be there) gaped. It would be the quickest wedding dress purchase in the history of wedding dresses, a staggering fifteen seconds.

"Maybe you should try on another one, just to be sure," my mom suggested.

"No," I said. "I want this one." I thought it was reasonably priced and didn't want to drag the process out.

My mother suggested we move on to the bridesmaid dresses, but this too was contentious because I wanted the bridesmaids to wear whatever they wanted.

"Why must everyone match?" I asked.

"Why are you such a pain in the ass?" my sister shot back. "No, really, tell me why." What she meant was, *Why must everything be a statement?*

But to me, the statement was the whole point. My wedding

was becoming a demonstration of all the things P.J. and I were not. The dresses, the napkins, the seating charts seemed an initiation into a domestic life that frightened me, one I had observed as a child and had sworn never to take part in. The wedding was an opportunity to declare, most of all to myself, that I could live according to whatever rules I wanted.

So when a Cuisinart was delivered to our apartment, my stomach dropped. It wasn't going to be that kind of marriage. My uncle had given us matching camping backpacks, and I had found that gift extremely gratifying. It aligned with the person I wanted to be: someone on the move, ready to jet off to some exciting adventure at barely a moment's notice, someone unencumbered.

Yet if I truly hadn't wanted the Cuisinart, I would have given it away. Instead I left it in its box above the kitchen cabinets, where I eyed it with suspicion and, occasionally, longing. Domestic objects had a mysterious power over me. I was both attracted to them and repulsed by them. The Cuisinart was sort of beautiful, with its sleek metal base. It promised homemade salsas and soft serve made of bananas and Nutella. How bad can life be when you are making your own soft serve?

I purged my life of household items with fervor. In limiting my exposure to them, I was hoping to cauterize the desire at its source. The longing for a beautiful teacup would never be satisfied by buying just one teacup. Once I had it, I would want some other beautiful thing, setting off a chain of longing and acquisition that would drag down my whole life. Even a single day spent around the house made me nearly frantic. I worried that I could, without realizing it, build a domestic life and become mired in it. So I renounced it all. No beautiful teacups ever.

Other kinds of household items—the ones you need in order to live—filled me with joy. I enjoyed seeing my toothbrush beside P.J.'s, his shoes mixed in with mine. I enjoyed grocery shopping with him, knowing that he liked the grainy mustard more than the smooth kind, the hard cheeses more than Brie. I felt the seductive appeal of controlling my surroundings, of nesting among picturesque things.

I told myself that it didn't matter if I was ambivalent about the wedding because I wasn't ambivalent about P.J. And though I didn't want to admit it, I craved the security of marriage. A handsome, kind man had agreed to tie his life to mine, to mix his shoes in with mine, to grocery shop with me, to list my name on his emergency contact forms forever. It was a vote of confidence in me and in my vision of how to live. The comfort that this knowledge provided released me from the pressure to find other forms of stability. I started taking on more ambitious writing projects because if they didn't work out I would still have P.J. I could live anywhere in the world because P.J. would be there. We had very little money, but being broke with someone else is far preferable to being broke alone. Surely between the two of us we would figure out how to make enough money to scrape by. I did not view my impending marriage as a constraint. I told myself that it was a means of escape from the constraints of the rest of the world.

On the Thursday night before the wedding, my side of the family began to arrive for a casual dinner at my parents' house. On the other side of town, P.J.'s aunts and uncles were beginning to arrive at his parents' house. Friends and family were settling into hotel rooms, guest bedrooms, and pullout couches. They came from Arkansas and California, South Korea and England. They took trains, planes, and buses. My parents' living room was abuzz with eager chatter and the sound of clinking glasses. My dad set up a cocktail bar in the study, and I stood beside P.J. talking to his best friend from college. In the living room, my aunt from England was perched on the couch laughing with one of P.J.'s groomsmen. A group stood by the mantel talking animatedly. The woman who babysat me as a toddler was there. The doorbell rang and more friends and family were hugged and ushered in. Their coats were added to an enormous heap on my parents' bed. My mother's best china and wineglasses covered every table and lap. The dog skittered from room to room, hoping that someone would drop a morsel of food.

I was moved. I had thought that the wedding was only about P.J. and me, and now I understood that it was also about everyone we knew. I had previously been embarrassed at the idea that people were traveling for our sakes, but now I saw that it wasn't about us, but about a group of friends and two families coming together. I had acted as if this wedding were a burden and now I was ashamed at my ingratitude. I had been afraid of something, but standing in the living room that night, I suddenly couldn't recall what it was.

The morning of the wedding, I woke up in my childhood bedroom feeling alert. The sky outside my window was a sharp, autumnal blue. Something large was about to happen. My parents' kitchen was filled with the flowers we had arranged the day before, and my uncles, cousin, and dad were whisking them off to the reception hall. The wedding party and I drove to the town hall, where the ceremony would be held, and I put on the dress, the first one I had tried on. A friend's mother who was acting as the ceremony coordinator had left snacks on a table with a sign that read: "No hypoglycemia on wedding day!" The room was a flutter of people putting on makeup and taking pictures. My little niece sat in my lap while I drank a beer. I bickered with my mom about whether I should be having a beer before the ceremony and then felt bad for snapping at her. Just beyond the door, I could hear people gathering in the hall.

Before I knew it, P.J.'s cousin started playing the violin. The wedding procession marched out, leaving my dad and me alone in the room. We were rarely overtly affectionate, preferring joking to outright displays of love, but the moment called for him to say something profound and fatherly.

"Everyone keeps asking me if I'm sad," he said, blushing. "I don't understand. Am I supposed to be sad?"

"No," I told him. But I wondered if he realized the reason why he wasn't sad. My mom once told me that on strolls around the neighborhood when I was a toddler, I would make her walk on the other side of the street, saying, "I walk by myself." As she told this story, I thought I detected a note of pride in her voice, but also of loss. Her toddler hadn't wanted to be near her—not because of anything she had done, but because of something constitutional.

When I went to dinner at friends' houses, I pretended I was their daughter, that they were my sisters and brothers, preferring my many imagined lives to the singular weight of one family. How could one family, one life lived in one place ever satisfy? I slept over at friends' houses on most weekends and played outside until dark on weeknights and this thrilled me. But I also knew that my insistence on independence had hurt people. Maybe my dad wasn't sad because he felt he had never really had me.

"I'm glad you're not sad," I said. "There's no reason to be."

I took his arm and opened the doors. Inside the cozily lit room were over a hundred people sitting close together, and there was P.J. at the front. I walked toward him. Everyone stood. A roomful of hushed people rising in unison, all of that brushing fabric, is a beautiful sound.

FOUR

Why would a little girl want to run away from a perfect child-hood? Barbara intended the world outside to be the house without windows, the place she was running to, but every time I read the title, I imagined someone in a windowless box banging on the walls, twisting the doorknobs, and trying to get out. According to her parents, Barbara already had her freedom—so why was she so obsessed with escape?

While combing through the Folletts' accounts of Barbara's childhood, I came across an inconsistency. It has to do with how Barbara learned to type. She did nearly all her writing on her typewriter, and her father hypothesized that this was what allowed her to communicate so eloquently at so young an age. It is easier to type than to labor over handwriting when your hands are small and not particularly dexterous. Barbara's mastery of the typewriter enabled her to write stories so exquisite that they broke the hearts of adults. That was Wilson's theory, at least.

The first account of Barbara's learning to type is from an article Wilson wrote for *Harper's* magazine. Then one day in the archives at Columbia University I came across Helen's account in an essay on Barbara's education that ran in *The Parents' Magazine* in 1932. In her version of the story, Barbara was five—a more believable age than Wilson's three. Helen says Barbara came up *to her, not Wilson,* and said, "Tell me a story about it."

Whose version is true? Barbara's father was more commonly at his typewriter, but her mother was around more. Barbara was almost impossibly young in Wilson's account, but then again, she was academically precocious.

There are, in many accounts of child prodigies, elements of wishful thinking, exaggerations, and sometimes even outright lies. Wilson and Helen had likely heard the story of William Sidis, the child prodigy mathematician who attended Harvard at age eleven and gave a lecture on the fourth dimension to a small group of slack-jawed mathematicians at the Harvard Mathematical Club. He was roughly Barbara's contemporary, fifteen years her senior, and after he died his sister claimed he had the highest IQ ever recorded—which is strange considering that there is no evidence he ever took an IQ test. There was no doubt that Sidis was remarkably smart, a genius by all accounts, but even he was not immune from adults' desires to embellish an already fantastic story.

In adulthood, Sidis would battle for control over his story, suing the *New Yorker* for libel over an article entitled "Where Are They Now?" about the boy genius's fall from grace. The magazine described his lonely later years, "living in . . . Boston's shabby end." If onlookers had originally rejoiced in elevating him, they now delighted in tearing him down. His complaint contended that the article had caused him "grievous mental anguish [and] humiliation." Sidis wanted to be left alone, to see himself as he wished to be seen. Seven years later, he won a settlement.

Wilson tried to temper his enthusiasm about Barbara's talents, claiming in *Harper's* that she was not a prodigy or a genius but "an example, as it seems to us and to others who know her, of absolute and beautiful normality in mind, disposition, and body." It was her education that had allowed her to flourish, he argued. But he may not have been able to resist small embellishments, turning a five-year-old typist into a three-year-old, and casting himself in the role of master teacher, to make her story—*his* story—a little grander.

What matters more than whether Barbara was three or five when she learned to type is that both parents had claimed the moment as theirs. Their vying affections, their expectations, may have been the burden she wanted to escape. Expectations certainly became a burden for William Sidis, so much so that he became estranged from his parents and recoiled entirely from the public eye. He began collecting streetcar transfers and rarely engaged in mathematics. He took the civil service exam but got a low score and died of a cerebral hemorrhage at the age of forty-six.

To be loved as ardently as Helen and Wilson appear to have loved Barbara is life affirming and confidence building. No wonder she felt she could tear off into the wild: she was constantly reminded that she was strong and capable. But such love can also be suffocating, especially if you want to be the one telling your own story. *The person in the room wishes to be left alone.* Barbara's desire to be productive was almost feverish and could make her surly. She once scolded a playmate: "You don't understand why I have my work to do—because, at this particular time, you have none at all." When your work matters to you a great deal, and people seem to be interfering, it's easy to see how life-affirming love could transform into the "gigantic burden" that Eepersip was relieved to escape. "We watch you," Wilson wrote in his baby book entry to Barbara. "She would be invisible forever" might have been her answer.

Parents technically can't divorce children, but they can and sometimes do abandon them. We will never know the full extent to which Wilson shaped his daughter's novel, but even if it was just on the sentence level, some part of Wilson may have yearned to see Eepersip vanish—to undo his perfect child.

Barbara's parents were demanding, and she made demands of her own. While most parents shuttle their children off to school and let someone else worry about the finer details of their education, Barbara's parents felt they had to constantly innovate in order to challenge their insatiably curious daughter. Then, when her lessons were over, she wanted her favorite playmate: her father. Wilson had literary ambitions of his own and a demanding editorial career. He meant to write a novel. But as he stated in his *Harper's* article, "It may be best in the long run to pour yourself into your child, as we are trying to do." Did pouring himself into Barbara feel like an act of self-obliteration?

Wilson's love was complicated. In one of the early baby book entries, he refers to himself as Barbara's "most unsparing critic." She was one year old. There is another passage in which he describes his desire to understand Barbara's baby talk: "We admire, we gloat, we adore, we worship—but O! how we want to understand! Perhaps you are the sole being in our cosmos whom to understand perfectly would be not to love less." Wilson preferred love at a distance. Intimacy diminished love's power.

Barbara wasn't Wilson's first child. He had another daughter, Grace, from an earlier marriage. When Grace's mother died in childbirth, Wilson sent Grace to live with his mother. He hardly ever saw her. A relative would later say of their relationship, "They were acquainted, but remotely." Perhaps he sent her away because she was a painful reminder of his wife's death; perhaps he blamed her for it. Barbara knew about Grace. Did she worry that her father's love for her could chill as well—that he might also banish her from his life? What if Barbara wanted to run away because it was easier to leave than to be left?

When Barbara was thirteen, she persuaded her parents to let her work for ten days as a ship hand aboard a three-masted schooner that sailed to Nova Scotia. She had just published her novel to great acclaim and was feeling emboldened. She could do anything adults could do. Wilson thought it would be an excellent adventure, and Helen alternated between fearing for her safety and not wanting her to wear her hair in braids. At sea Barbara learned to steer the ship and tie the ropes. She memorized the points of the compass, climbed all over the rigging, practiced her pirate slang, and chatted with the sailors about how much it cost to get a tooth pulled on the mainland. When she went ashore with one of her sailor friends her only regret was not getting a tattoo.

One day there was a storm. The rumbling of the swiftly gathering clouds, the sudden temperature drop, the way that everyone stopped what they were doing captivated her and "crowded all feelings out of you except the feeling of its awesome self." She was experiencing that exquisite mixture of awe and terror, an awareness of one's own fragility before the ever-churning immensity of nature. One lightning snap, one roaring wave could snatch you from life forever. How beautiful to be here, to feel the crack of lightning as if it were in your bones, to hear the waves crash against the hull—but to live. She wanted to remember this feeling forever.

The photographs of Barbara at sea are the ones in which she looks her most daring—and most satisfied. In one she is standing on a ship's deck in knickers and a sailor's cap, her hands on her hips, with a defiant expression. She spent the ten days in a kind of manic ecstasy. The adventures she had dreamed up were finally coming true. It was as though Eepersip had leapt off the page. She came back with enough material to fill another book and wrote it in a white-hot heat. Her account of her time at sea, *The Voyage of the Norman D.,* was published, also by Knopf, to rave reviews when she was fourteen. Her literary career was all but guaranteed. But the voyage had made her hungry for more—perhaps insatiably so.

The year Barbara's second book came out, Wilson was working closely with Alfred Knopf, the charismatic cofounder of the Knopf publishing house. It was an exciting time to be in publishing. Though Knopf was a relatively young operation, it had a reputation for refined literary taste, thanks in part to the discerning eye of Blanche Knopf, Alfred's wife and partner. The Knopfs were publishing authors like D. H. Lawrence, E. M. Forster, and Somerset Maugham, and they seemed to have a knack for identifying the books that would move people and shape the culture. Later, Alfred Knopf would write, "I believe I have never published an unworthy book." Wilson had a good rapport with Alfred, who in turn seemed to be invested in Wilson's future. He trusted Wilson's judgment. Wilson had a promising career ahead of him.

The demanding nature of his job meant that Wilson was spending more time in New York, away from his family. His absences particularly upset Barbara, who wrote: "Nothing ever happens unless you're here." Helen might have been the engine that made the family run, but Wilson was the spark. He was Barbara's co-conspirator, her writing muse, the one whose praise she most longed for. Life was drab without him. He needed to be in the woods with her, not traipsing around in the concrete world, stuck in a sun-starved, seventh-floor office on Fifth Avenue.

Just before Barbara left for her sea voyage, she had written him a letter and told him so.

Dear Daddy,
*   It seems to us that New York must be a sort of Louis XI's*
palace full of snares, temptations, pit-falls, traps, and
everything else for enticing and entangling its helpless victims.
But now we have a stunning excuse for you to come home.

During one of her solo excursions near the cottage the family rented every summer in New Hampshire, Barbara had discovered a brick wall at the top of a hill, which was overgrown with enormous violets and foliage: "I intend to make a great many visits, basket and shovel in hand, to this veritable Eden-of-cultivated-things-gone-wild, and I hope you will come along." She saw her father's work as a distraction from the place where he truly belonged: in nature with her.

One night, the phone rang at two in the morning in the Follett house. Wilson picked up, and Helen listened.

"I tried to, but I couldn't," he said to the person on the other end.

What Wilson was trying to do was tell Helen that he had met someone, a younger someone. Margaret Whipple also worked at

Knopf and sat at the desk next to his. She was twenty years old, which made her just six years older than Barbara. Wilson wanted to leave his family to be with her.

Barbara found this out in a letter that arrived on her fourteenth birthday, in March. She was frantic. She thought her father had lost his mind. Knowing that he was logical and unsentimental, she made a logical appeal to him rather than a sentimental one. They had *plans,* she argued. He couldn't possibly leave them when they were supposed to go hiking in Maine and boating on Lake Sunapee. The argument was not, *Don't leave me because I love you.*

Wilson telephoned the house and spoke to Barbara. He was reassuring. "Hold your horses," he told her. "Everything will be all right." Barbara brightened. The only possible interpretation of "everything will be all right" was that he would reconsider and come home. He knew that Sabra, who was only four, needed him. He knew that Barbara needed him. She let this idea console her.

But the next day, a letter arrived that made it clear he was not coming back. He told Barbara that his marriage to her mother was poisonous and destructive and that it had always been this way. Barbara had to admit she had noticed a strain in the last year, but not always. He was rewriting history, and Barbara was furious. She saw now that he had deceived her on the telephone. His reassurances were part of his plan to keep her out of the way while he went off plotting a new life without her.

Barbara and Sabra were playing at a neighbor's house when their mother telephoned and told them to come home. When Barbara got to the house, she found Margaret Whipple in their living room. Margaret wanted to speak to Barbara alone. She was pretty, in a sharp, angular way, and wore her blond hair loosely collected in a bun. She had a long, elegant neck. Barbara eyed her suspiciously.

It's not clear why Helen granted her husband's mistress a private meeting with her fourteen-year-old daughter, or why Margaret thought it was appropriate to ask. Perhaps Margaret saw that Barbara held more sway with Wilson than Helen did. It was a strategic move to get the blessing of the beloved daughter. Barbara recorded what followed in a letter to her father.

Margaret began soothingly. "You see, Barbara, I think he would be happy and contented with me; and you wouldn't object to his being happy and contented, would you?"

"You think you can make him happy?" Barbara asked.

"I do," said Margaret.

"Well, but is that a very honorable sort of happiness?"

"I don't know; you see, I suppose I'm in love with him."

"Well, then I think you ought to try and get out of love just as quick as ever you can. Besides, can't you be on friendly, happy terms with him, without taking him away from his family?"

Margaret was baffled. The daughter was worse than the mother. "People in love just don't do that—that's all."

"Then what do you want; what do you expect?"

"I want to marry him."

"Yes; but I might raise objections to that."

Margaret tried another tactic. "You see, your mother told me that if I married him I'd ruin your whole life, smash all your ideals, and all that. Well, I don't want to do that; you may not believe it, but I don't. Would it ruin your whole life?"

It must have been tempting to say yes, but Barbara's reply was remarkably reasonable under the circumstances. "I don't see how I can tell whether it would or not. It might not ruin the whole of it; but don't you see?—it isn't that—it's simply the fact that it's dishonorable and unfair, that's all. Good heavens, Miss Whipple—don't you see what you're doing? Can even you, 'in love,' as you say, think that it is fair to take a man away from his family as you're doing? You can realize that you are not in the right of it, can't you."

"Unfortunately, I'm not," Margaret said.

"Indeed, and I think it's extremely fortunate that you're not. Besides, do you want to know what I think? I suppose you don't, but here it is, anyhow: I think you've taken an unfair advantage of him when he was and is in a physically low condition—exhausted with work, powerless to resist your 'love,' as you call it. Because I can tell you I am absolutely sure that, if he were in his right mind, he would never think of such a thing—never even listen to it for a minute."

Margaret shrugged in defeat. Just then, Helen came into the room. Margaret turned to Helen and said, "Well, Barbara's been trying to give me advice."

"You can't blame her," Helen said sharply. "She's only fourteen, and she's having her father taken away from her."

A taxi arrived for Margaret, but Barbara couldn't contain herself any longer. She moved in closer and said menacingly, "Besides, I have another thing to say to you, and it's this: If I were in the painful position you're in; if I were doing what you are trying your best to do, I wouldn't stand up there, so extremely unashamed of myself."

"Thank you," Margaret said mockingly. "That's all I can think of to say." She got up to leave.

"Good-bye, Miss Whipple," Barbara said. "I'm going to swear at you behind your back when you've gone."

Barbara had outmaneuvered her father's mistress and made her feel like a fool. She had the nerve to fight for what she believed in. She was unfolding her wings, flexing her muscles.

The letter to her father was much more than an attempt to showcase her debating talents. She hoped to convince him to come home. It was nearly spring in New Haven, just the season when her father missed the mountain air most. If she could paint the picture of the two of them tramping around together in the woods, she might lure him back. The letter begins:

> *Dear Daddy,*
>
> *I did receive your letter, yesterday afternoon, and I read it (as you must suppose) a good many times before I came to any conclusion or conclusions concerning it. . . .*
>
> *Aren't we ever again going to cross ranges of mountains in all weathers, or play about in Sternway, or steer a real windjammer through the seven seas, or take sailing-lessons from Mr. Rasmussen—as we once planned?*
>
> *Such things do not reconcile themselves. For instance, if you now finally and determinedly drop all that, leave it behind, kick it out of the way, then how am I to believe that they actually and truly meant all to you that they seemed to at the time? And if they did, then how am I to believe that you don't feel any more the lure of The Maine Woods—the lure of*

that mountain that we have always had vaguely in our minds? . . .

I depend very much on you; and I trust you to give another heave to the capstan bars, to get the family anchor started toward the surface again. After all, you have the strongest shoulders for heaving of us all!

The letter didn't work.

Barbara had dedicated *The House Without Windows* to her father as well as to Sabra, and now he wanted nothing to do with their adventures. He was on his own adventure without her, and she was arguing against wild impulses, coaxing him to come home. In that moment, she didn't want freedom. She wanted her family.

In the months after her father's departure, Barbara was drawn to people who gave her absolute assurance of their devotion. She had found it at sea among the ship hands, sea captains, and cooks she met during her Nova Scotia voyage, and she corresponded hungrily with them after her father left. "Sailors are the most delightful beings on earth," she wrote. They swapped stories about their drunken shipmates, tyrannical captains, gales, and shipwrecks. "Dear Shipmate," "Dearest Shipmate," "Hail Shipmate," their letters read.

The Follett home was becoming an increasingly unhappy place and Barbara was itching to return to sea. Helen was constantly fending off Wilson's requests for a divorce. At night, she hardly slept. One morning Sabra wandered into the kitchen and asked her mother, "When is Daddy coming home? He's been gone for so long." Helen couldn't tell her that the answer was never, just as she couldn't tell either of her daughters her darker secret: that she blamed them for Wilson's leaving.

"They have been the cause of my losing him," she wrote to Anne, a close friend of the Folletts. Helen had dedicated her life to Barbara and Sabra, forsaking her own ambitions, and she had felt the burn of that sacrifice long before Wilson left her. "It's a pity mothers are [such] busy people," she had written in the baby book when Barbara was three, "it's a pity they can't leave the ugly details of dish washing, floor cleaning and all the rest to Mrs. O'Neil and those who love the sloshing sloppy water; it's a pity mothers can't do what they want to."

Helen's resentment of her children reached fever pitch after Wilson left. "I am frightfully jealous of the person who has usurped my place," she wrote to Anne, "the particular place I have always longed for—of living with him and writing alone. I think, perhaps, it all accounts for my indifference to the children. . . . Without him, they seem to touch me so vaguely." She added, "I do promise, however, not to dump them on the world without taking adequate justification."

A few months later she wrote, "The farther away I am from homes, families, houses that resemble my own—the happier I am." There was, it seems, a little bit of Eepersip in all of the Folletts.

Helen begged Wilson to be a part of the children's lives, even if he wouldn't be a part of hers. They needed him, she insisted— Barbara especially. Didn't he care that Barbara felt betrayed?

Wilson wrote back, "As to Barbara: I will tell you again, as I have always told you, that I'm not going to be party to any competition for her attention or affection. Her attitude of whole-hearted support of your position and hostility to mine is exactly what I most wish it to be, and I wouldn't for anything in the world curry any sort of favor with her." Wilson didn't want Barbara on his side because he didn't want her in his life. He didn't want to be responsible for caring for the girls at all: "They must go with you, be yours," he wrote. If Barbara was angry at him, so much the better. Then she would leave him alone.

If Barbara had wanted to run away before, now she had justification. A house in which one parent was conspicuously absent and the other miserable and blaming you for the end of her marriage could very quickly become a place that a child might want to flee.

And so she did.

In June, about three months after Wilson left the family, Barbara took the train to see him in the redbrick row house he was renting with Margaret on Perry Street in Greenwich Village. It's not clear exactly what transpired, as the only record of this visit is a brief mention in a letter Helen wrote to a friend. Helen reported that Wilson was cold and indifferent to Barbara and that Barbara was stunned. The next morning, back in New Haven, Barbara didn't come downstairs for breakfast. Helen went to her room to check on her and saw that she hadn't slept in her bed. She panicked.

Barbara had snuck out of the house at three in the morning and walked in the dark for three miles. It was a straight shot down Prospect Street to Union Station. She was a shape moving in the darkness, passing under oak trees, in and out of the moonlight, past the darkened colonial homes in which people were fast asleep. Being out and about in the cool night air while the rest of the world sleeps is exhilarating, an excitement tinged with danger. Eventually, she arrived at the train station, a grand, hulking brick structure with large arched windows. She caught the four o'clock train. She would ride it for sixty miles to Pelham, New York, to stay with family friends. When the engine lurched into motion and emerged from the sleepy predawn town, she must have felt a little giddy. She could leave too.

She came home a few days later, but by then Helen was despairing, sensing that the trouble was only just beginning. "You have no idea how she has changed," she wrote to Anne. "She declares she has as much right to her freedom as her father has to his." Wilson's departure had awakened something in Barbara, something jagged and dark—a need to run.

Helen decided to take the girls to the cottage on Lake Sunapee alone that summer. Friends would be there and it would be good to get away from the family house on Armory Street. One day, Wilson showed up at the cottage to discuss a divorce. He and Helen fought bitterly. Barbara was tired of these "Family Scenes," as she had begun to call them. She walked out of the cottage to float on a raft in the lake. Lying on the raft, looking out at the wooded peninsulas, the rocks and pines that lined the shore, and the sun sparkling on the water, Barbara suddenly understood something. The universe was huge, and Lake Sunapee was just a speck in it. *God must have to use a microscope,* she thought. She was small, her parents were small, and everything they worried or thought about was small. Why couldn't they see what she saw? She felt lucky, lying on her raft in the lake, not being drawn into such trivial things. The world was beautiful and they were missing it. It would all be over before they knew it.

During this period Barbara developed some cynical ideas about marriage. It was the antithesis of freedom, and freedom mattered most. Not long after her father left, she discovered that one of her sailor friends was getting married. She was outraged and wrote him a scathing letter: "You must not, *you must not,* YOU MUST NOT! Don't you understand, mad shipmate? Where's your freedom now, where will it be later? Where the mad adventures . . . we won't look at you with a wife." She signed her letter, "Your enraged shipmate, Blackheart."

It was only natural that the end of her parents' marriage had made her jaded. Why would someone give up the camaraderie of shipmates for something so flimsy as marriage? On some level her rejection of marriage and staunch support of adventure was a defense of her father, even if only subconsciously. He wasn't a deserter; he just had an adventurous soul. She was straining to reconcile the fact that the very thing she loved most about him— his ferocious defense of freedom—had caused her to lose him. After the incident when she visited him and Margaret on Perry Street, Barbara was rarely in touch with him. Part of her still admired her father and wanted to be loved by him, though outwardly she claimed otherwise.

Her divided heart comes through in her letters. In one she writes, "He isn't exactly what you'd call a Man." She called Margaret and Wilson "the Farents," likely a merging of "Folletts" and "parents," though one could just as easily imagine the *F* standing for "fake" or "far." Barbara wrote, "I know nothing of them and I really don't care a damn now." But two months later, she couldn't help but ask a family friend, "Have you seen or heard anything from the Farents? I confess a mild sort of curiosity."

One night she told her mother, "You know I used to pretend I didn't care, but I did care more than anyone will ever know." Over the next decade, she would hardly see him at all.

Barbara was developing a philosophy, the root of which contained a contradiction. Everyone should do exactly as they please and run off to the mountains whenever the mood struck them, but they should also be unerringly loyal. She had written, "There should be nothing to make a man or a woman happier than a pack of real honest-to-goodness friends, who will always stand by you in your troubles of which you are sure to have many." In the real world, complete loyalty is hard enough to find, all the more so paired with its opposite—total freedom. But Barbara fervently embraced these two warring ideas.

Wilson's letters to Helen were becoming increasingly desperate. He must have his freedom, he said. He was anxious to put his marriage behind him so he could create a new life with Margaret. At one point, he threatened to disappear: "And if I am left in my present situation I shall really be forced out of my house and connections and into disappearance from the same." Helen told a friend that she was worried he would vanish or commit suicide if she didn't give him a divorce but that she would sooner let him do that.

And then Wilson did disappear. In June, Alfred Knopf fired him. The affair was indecent. There had been gossip, and Alfred felt he couldn't trust Wilson's judgment anymore. Alfred knew Helen and the children and told Wilson he had until August 15 to go. Shortly before that, Helen had come to New York to see Alfred. It's not clear what they discussed. The fact that Wilson was fired not long afterward suggests that she may have had something to do with it. Perhaps her meeting was a final attempt to get Wilson back. Or perhaps she knew their marriage was a lost cause and the meeting was purely vindictive. She had lost everything. Perhaps he should too.

Whatever her plan, it mostly backfired. Wilson wrote to Helen, "My career as Wilson Follett is done." He went on to say that he had every intention of supporting her and the girls, though obviously it would be harder to do now that he didn't have income. His only hope of getting a reputable job was to marry Margaret. Couldn't Helen see that this was in her own interest? "I have been extremely ill and feeble," he groveled. He was "in that condition in which a man is likely to go pathetic."

Meanwhile Barbara received five hundred dollars from *Harper's* to sail around the Caribbean and the South Seas for a year and write about her adventure. In a last-ditch effort to wrench Wilson from Margaret, Helen suggested that he go with Barbara.

"My whole instinct and wish the instant I can shed New York will be to head north not south," Wilson responded emphatically. "I've responsibilities other than financial which wouldn't be at all well served by my running away with Barbara . . . To this much I might add that if by spectacular luck I should get abreast of the financial difficulties with any margin of ease to spare, I should want to use the margin to make something of myself after all these years . . . I don't put myself first, but I don't see any reason for not putting myself next after the discharge of my material obligations."

The matter was settled. If Wilson was going to start his life over again, Barbara and Helen would too. Helen sent four-year-old

Sabra to stay with a family friend, Margaret Tyler, in New Haven and told Barbara she would join her on her journey. Wilson, Helen said, was allowed to visit Sabra at Margaret Tyler's, but he was not to take her to his apartment with Margaret in New York. She told Anne that should she die on the trip, she wanted her to arrange for Sabra's care. Before Helen left, she considered burning the letters between her and Wilson. "You see we were never away from each other without a daily letter," she wrote to Anne. But she couldn't bring herself to do it. "I want Bar and Sabra to know something of the greatness that was so fine and is so rare."

On September 15, Barbara and Helen boarded the S.S. *Voltaire,* a steamship in New York that was bound for Barbados. They had a suitcase and a typewriter each. Sabra and her new guardian came to wave them off. Wilson was not there. On October 8, Helen wrote to Anne, "And I want Sabra! This is the first time I have dared to think of her!" Sabra and Helen would not be reunited for nearly a year and a half. Prolonged absences from children were more common then, but still the decision to leave such a young child for a year is striking.

Wilson swore he would send them money every month, but according to Helen, he didn't. Instead, he vanished. Helen wrote frantic letters to friends trying to discover his whereabouts. His letters stopped coming. No one, it seemed, knew where he was.

A year later, when Helen and Barbara returned to the United States, Helen arranged for Barbara, who was now fifteen, to live in Pasadena, California, with friends of the family, while Helen went to Honolulu. She was writing a book about her and

Barbara's time at sea and following a lead on a museum job there. Helen thought it might be best for both of them if they spent some time apart. They had quarreled viciously during the voyage— Barbara insisting on her independence, and Helen grasping for a modicum of control. For the first time in Barbara's life, she was sent to school with kids her own age.

She lasted no more than a couple of weeks. "I was not given the conventional upbringing and it is too late to try to standardize me now," she told a reporter.

She dashed off a handwritten letter to her mother in Honolulu. "I'm not going to tell you, for the time being, where I'll be; and names, jobs, and headquarters have all been completely changed, you see. So we're unfindable. Besides, I want to be alone with my Disillusion or my Fairytale—as the case may be. And I expect I'll be seeing you again in this incarnation."

She was fifteen and could create a new name, find a job and a place to live. Identity was fluid. She could be something else entirely later.

But who was this "we"? *We're unfindable.* During the voyage, Helen had alluded to Barbara spending time with "a Scotchman . . . her father's age." Barbara had become infatuated with him, and this had concerned Helen, though there's no suggestion that he felt even remotely the same. Alternatively, she could have been lying.

When the police found her, however, she was alone. She had taken a train from Los Angeles to San Francisco, where she hid in a boardinghouse under an assumed name: K. Andrews. When the police came to the door, she tried to climb out the boarding-house window, but they grabbed her before she could escape. When Helen's friends who were acting as Barbara's guardians in Pasadena arrived to pick her up from the police station, she protested so much that the police decided to keep her in their custody until a guardian more to her liking could be found.

The press had a field day, calling her "the young literary genius." She gave several interviews, and the stories ran under headlines like "Child Writer in Revolt," "Girl Novelist to Be Kept at Juvenile Hall," and "Runaway Authoress Returned." In one she explained calmly, "I am told that I am wanted in the South for forging a check. Well, I might do anything else, even murder, for there is a streak of crime in my nature, but I didn't do that." The journalist who recorded her statement noted the pride in her tone. To have a streak of crime in your nature was adventurous, if not downright glamorous. But in the dozens of articles about Barbara's running away, I found no mention of this forged check, which made me wonder if she had made it up. She was, after all, devoted to storytelling, hungrily seeking to fill her life with as many adventurous tales as she could. In her stories, she was always the brave heroine, willing to go anywhere and do anything.

Before the police found her, Barbara had hoped to get a job as a secretary. If that wasn't possible, she would work as a waitress or a clerk. All the while, she would hone her writing skill. "I know that I couldn't support myself by my writing yet," she told a journalist, "but I could be perfecting it, seeking real criticism and development." She ended the interview by saying, "That is the life I planned for myself, and all I ask is to be let alone to do what seems best to me."

But she was a minor and no one would leave her alone to do what seemed best for her. Barbara awaited her hearing in a prison cell. There were four little girls in matching blue school uniforms in the cell next to her, which she called a cage. She told a reporter that looking at them made her wonder, "Why are older people crushing us in this way? It seems to me I cannot wait six whole years until I am twenty-one in order just to be free."

FIVE

A year before our wedding, P.J. and I decided we needed to get out of D.C. Leaving would mean saying good-bye to nearly everyone we knew, which was, at least to me, exactly the point. Wanting to flee, if only for a time, is a fairly common fantasy. Anyone who has felt it will recognize that this feeling manages to coexist with the fact that you may love your friends and family very much. *I love you. Please go away.*

Many of our friends from our respective high schools, our college friends, our parents, and P.J.'s siblings and their combined five children lived within a five-mile radius of our home. There was an endless string of birthdays, happy hours, going-away or coming-home parties, soccer games, holiday and engagement parties. I often felt that rather than trying to actually spend time together in a meaningful way, we were crossing things—or people—off our to-do lists.

The total lack of spontaneity was making me fidgety. In college, I hadn't done extracurricular activities, even ones I would have enjoyed, because I didn't like the idea that I would have to agree to weekly meetings. As a result, I spent a lot of nights doing nothing when I could have been doing something constructive; but knowing I was free to do as I pleased was what I cared about most. Now I knew ahead of time what I would be doing every weekend for the next five months. I dreamed of saying to family and friends, "I don't want to see you today because I need to be alone, or I need to write, or wander around without a plan, and that's not a reflection of how I feel about you."

I might have enjoyed the merry-go-round of social events more had I not been working so much. I was running my family's coffee shop, waking up at five in the morning to open the store in the dark, do inventory, organize and restock the line, brew coffee, order more, create the next week's schedule, and serve food and drinks all day. Often I had to cover shifts for employees who had overslept or were sick. On the rare occasion when I wasn't in the shop, my cell phone would ring incessantly with questions from the staff. "The sink is clogged and overflowing." "There's a crazy man shouting at himself in the bathroom." "We're out of peanut butter." "There's a weird smell coming from the basement." Each time my phone rang, it reminded me that I wasn't a good manager. I had created an environment where people were helpless in my absence.

At night I came home with my jeans stained with coffee grounds, worrying about two employees who were fighting or a tense interaction with a customer. I was physically exhausted, but when I got in bed, instead of going to sleep, I cycled through the next day's to-do list. We're out of whole milk, I reminded myself. And don't forget to order more bowls for the catering job next week. The new employee is coming in at eleven; print her paperwork first thing.

I was beginning to see that when your days are all the same, your weeks, months, and years blend together. The alumni association of my high school asked for an update for the school magazine and I didn't have one. "Nothing has changed," I imagined writing. "Laura Smith, Class of 2004, is exactly the same." I imagined that my classmates were climbing the Annapurna circuit, kayaking the length of the Nile, and rescuing earthquake victims in China. I longed to see other places. Even looking at a map was painful because it reminded me of how mired I was in my life. A National Geographic special about the pyramids came on, and I thought, *I really might never get to Egypt.* My world was small.

"When are you coming over?" my mother and P.J.'s would ask in rapid succession. "Let's get a date on the calendar for something this week."

"You're smothering me," I said to my mother.

"That sounds nice," I said to P.J.'s mother.

One night I looked into the bathroom mirror, feeling suddenly daunted by the task of flossing my teeth. How could I possibly bring myself to do one more thing I didn't want to do? I slept fitfully that night and had a dream that I had fallen asleep at a dinner party and was surrounded by an endless cacophony of cocktail chatter and clinking glasses. I had never spent less time reading or writing in my life, probably since I had learned to read and write, and the lack of it made my life feel lusterless. "My brain is dying," I told P.J. I was an automaton outputting work and taking in food and drink.

P.J. sometimes came in to help on the weekends, working behind the counter so I wouldn't have to. He was teaching at a nearby high school and was often up grading papers until the early hours of the morning, but he never complained about the extra work. He memorized the smoothie recipes and sometimes made them wrong. I didn't care because I was so grateful not to be the one making them.

His desire to please others was great when it worked in my favor. But when he wanted to please others at my expense I would grow irritated. "Of course we'll be there!" I heard him say into the phone. I shot him a death stare, signaling that I was going to strangle him. He shrugged helplessly, whispering, "If we leave the dinner at nine we can be at the birthday party just half an hour after it starts."

"Do you actually want to go?" I would ask him. Sometimes the answer was yes, sometimes it was no. When he would commit to things I didn't want to do, I wouldn't allow myself to blame him. It was the other person's fault. I didn't want to think about the fact that sometimes I felt trapped by him.

I wrote during any free moment I could get. After work, late at night, I would write in the darkness of our studio apartment while P.J. slept in the bed nearby. In between placing orders I wrote in the coffee shop's cavernous unfinished basement, which smelled like damp concrete. Sometimes I typed notes on my cell phone between shifts. But the moments snatched here and there were never enough. I could never really gather the intense concentration needed because I was constantly interrupted.

"I can't live without writing," a journalist friend told me. I rolled my eyes because the truth is that you *can* live without writing. In fact, often we *must* live without it.

If I wasn't writing, I was simmering with frustration about how I should be. At a bar with friends, even if I was having a good time, I would silently berate myself for again being lured away from my work. I wanted to write more than I wanted to be near the people I loved. Sometimes I worried that this made me smallhearted or selfish, but it seemed constitutional and therefore unlikely to change.

I began writing about a woman who disappears. Not Barbara, but a fictional woman. She was a botanist who had vanished, perhaps deliberately, in the Burmese jungle in search of a rare, psychedelic mushroom. I wrote about her because, of course, I wanted to disappear. Often those who write about women who have vanished are men with an impulse to eviscerate women, or women with an impulse to eviscerate themselves. I was interested in a different kind of vanishing: the kind where you disentangle yourself from your life and start fresh. People would miss you. You could miss them. You could live at a peaceful distance, loving them in a way that is simpler than the way you love someone you have to deal with in everyday life. You hadn't abandoned them. You were just gone. Mysterious rather than rejecting. Vanishing was a way to reclaim your life.

"Let's leave the country," P.J. said one night after work over burritos at a Mexican chain restaurant. We had been talking casually about moving abroad for a while, but the idea was tantalizing and somehow more urgent now that we were deep in the weeds of wedding planning. Moving away was another way to say no without having to say it. "Oh, I'm so sorry," I imagined myself saying. "We can't go to dinner because we'll be in Asia." We had talked about traveling, but never in a way that felt like more than daydreaming. But a few months earlier a local restaurant owner had offered to buy our coffee shop, at a loss of course, and my dad and I jumped at the opportunity to be rid of what had once been a dream. Without the coffee shop, P.J. and I could shed everything that had burdened us in D.C.

"Can we please?" I said.

"We can do whatever we want," P.J. said.

Two days after the wedding, P.J. and I were in his sister's basement frantically packing. A book I wanted was nowhere to be found, a friend was dropping by with a last-minute wedding present, and we were trying to figure out what to do with $130 in coins another friend had given us as a generous gag gift. We had a plane to catch, I had a stress rash on my face, and somehow in the post-wedding rush I had strained my neck, making it painful to turn my head to the right. We were moving to Southeast Asia for a year, mostly because it was the farthest away we could get on the planet before coming back around again. The weather, the people, the sounds and smells would all be new to us. Days would be remarkable again.

We had saved some money and had a few freelance writing and research contracts that could be done remotely. That money would cover our expenses, which would be minimal: we had picked Southeast Asia because it was cheap.

I ran upstairs, tore the cushions off the couch, didn't find the book, then ran downstairs to my backpack and started ripping out the clothing I had neatly rolled inside. Our backpacks contained everything we would need for the next year, which it turned out wasn't much. We'd each packed five shirts, two pairs of shorts, a pair of pants, and a couple of pairs of shoes. There were also our computers, books, and two notebooks. Other than knowing what I would wear for the next year, I had no real plan. Suddenly, I didn't care about the book. We were leaving, and how little our old lives would overlap with our new one was thrilling.

We drove to Dulles International Airport with our respective parents because both sets wanted to take us. P.J.'s sister and her children followed behind in their minivan. This vast crowd stood in a knot at the international departures area to watch us check in. At the check-in counter, something appeared to be wrong.

"You don't have return tickets?" the ticket taker asked.

"That's correct," P.J. said.

"What is your plan for exiting Thailand?"

"We'll be leaving by bus."

I turned around and looked at our families standing behind us. Their faces were hopeful. Had we botched the trip? Would we have to stay home forever?

A few months earlier, my mother-in-law had sat us down on her porch and said, "Maybe you should consider going away for a few months instead of a year." I felt something constrict in my chest. She seemed to be asking us not to change, or to get onto some kind of track. To her, this was a trip. We would come back to our apartment in D.C., back to her house for dinner on Sundays, to "regular" (i.e., office) jobs and daily routines. The coffee shop had been a nice little digression, but that hadn't turned out so well. Teaching—that was fine in your twenties, as long as it was a stepping-stone to something more prestigious. And now this "trip." It was time to grow up and get serious. This line of thinking made me want to run screaming in the opposite direction. I couldn't describe the life I wanted, but this was not it.

It was around this time that I read a passage in a novel about two old ladies, a mother and a daughter who lived alone together in some isolated place eating only potatoes. When a stranger came across them, he was struck by how the pair seemed to have withered mentally without outside stimulus. Having only each other to talk to, they were nearly mute. Without other minds, other sights, other experiences, they had grown dull. The passage had sent a jolt of fear through me. I was surrounded by people who loved me, people whom I loved, and yet I was wilting. I thought about Wilson Follett and the urgency he felt to end his "poisonous" marriage. Maybe Helen wasn't poisonous, but something about family life *was*. I didn't like the idea that I might be anything like Wilson, who was, in many ways, the villain of Barbara's story.

You must be vigilant, Wilson argued, because even the best-intentioned love can strangle. You cannot protect the things you love by sealing them in airtight containers. When you pin a butterfly and put it behind glass, you kill it. Barbara put her butterflies in a sieve, studied them, and then released them back into the wild. Go outside, she seemed to be saying. Be fearless, life will be over soon.

Barbara once signed a letter to her father, "With love and love and love and <u>love</u> and LOVE and <u>LOVE</u>," each inky love becoming larger and larger. When her father wasn't there, she wrote, "I am longing to see you" and "I miss you terribly." Where is the dividing line in a love like this? At some point, love crosses over from being the buoy that lifts you up to the tide that drags you under. My chest was pounding as I sat on the porch and P.J.'s mother asked us to stay, and it was pounding just as loudly in the airport as we tried to leave. Perhaps Wilson was just being who he was when he left his family. Maybe I was too. It wasn't a question of wrong or right or ingratitude. It was a compulsion.

Standing at the check-in counter, I imagined failing to get our boarding passes and piling back into the family cars. I could picture our mothers' looks of contented relief as we all drove home together. *Put us on that fucking airplane,* I thought.

"Listen," P.J. said to the agent, "if when we land in Thailand they want us to turn back around, we'll do that."

The woman shrugged and processed our tickets.

We were running away not just from home but from a certain idea of what married life should be. Marriage is in many ways freedom's opposite, the binding of one life to another—in theory at least—forever. So as I tied myself to P.J. with one hand, I untethered myself from the rest of my life—family, friends, my job, my apartment—with the other.

As the plane lifted off the tarmac, I felt I had escaped. But leaving the country for a year isn't that unusual. People quit their jobs and move all the time. They travel. It's an indulgence, but nothing truly revolutionary. Yet suspended in the night sky, surrounded by strangers reading, talking, and sleeping, I knew leaving meant much more than that. If you had asked me then what I would have been willing to risk to find freedom, I would have said everything—except P.J.

SIX

While Barbara and Helen sailed the Caribbean and the South Seas, Wilson was living on the coast of Maine, in Penobscot Bay, writing a novel, *No More Sea,* about seven generations of an adventure-loving seafaring family, also living in Penobscot Bay. Like Barbara, he was toying with his fantasies, letting some of what he put on the page bleed into real life and vice versa.

No More Sea is a story about vanishing men. Abel Teaswith, a sailor, comes to America from England in search of something that he can't describe but is certain is out there. When he arrives in Penobscot Bay, he sees two spruce-covered headlands "close around him like enfolding arms." The harbor's cove is lush with forest, dotted with wooden village houses. A white church steeple peeks through the dense fir and spruce trees. Abel smells the salt spray and feels the warm sunlight on his face. He builds a large house. Is this what happened when Wilson arrived in Penobscot Bay with Margaret? He looked around him and assured himself that yes, now he would finally be satisfied.

In the novel, this satisfaction lasts for seven generations. Abel's descendants do exactly as he did, setting off on long stints at sea and returning to their patient wives in the house that Abel had built. In this perpetual motion between home and sea, the

Teaswith men found the key to lasting satisfaction: "infinite variety within eternal unity." The variety was the sea. The unity was a beautiful home in a natural place surrounded by family. They had everything.

Yet nearly all the Teaswith men die at sea. This, Wilson writes, is their "inherited doom." Even though they know the sea will kill them, they prefer danger and certain death to "living by rote" and the "sleepwalker's trance" of the lawyers, bankers, and civil engineers eyed with scorn at various points in the book. They defend their dangerous lifestyle by arguing that though they might live longer doing something else, what would they be living *for*? "To let other men make your decisions for you, or worse yet, to be drifted into them by mere chance like a corpse in a tideway—that was to be as good as dead all your life." It is precisely because of the danger that the Teaswith men are so alive. Only by living on the edge of cataclysm could they feel death's opposite.

The book can be read as an elaborate justification for Wilson's abandonment of his family. The Teaswith men are blameless rascals, victims of "a tragic ancestral pattern" that would be futile to resist. After Luella's husband dies at sea, her grandmother tells her, "He did the only thing there was to do, he being the man he was." A good Teaswith woman, Wilson writes, is "enduring and steadfast, acquainted with loneliness, grateful for whatever compensations there might be, and silent about all that is asked to be compensated." In short, a good woman keeps quiet and doesn't interfere with her husband's adventuring. In passage after passage, Wilson argues that the women who stand in the way are to blame—not the men who leave.

If Barbara's novel is occasionally dissatisfying because we don't understand Eepersip's motives, Wilson's suffers from too much logic. He had the abandonment of two families to justify, and *No More Sea* collapses under the weight of his desire to fit his impulses into a neat rationale. There are moments, though, when he stops moralizing and stares at his impulses nakedly. Flipping through the pages, I began to feel an uncomfortable sensation: recognition. Restlessness may seem at first glance to be a problem of indecision—hopping from one place to the next, one job to the next, one lover to the next. But the restless people in Wilson's story are actually remarkably decisive, only their decisions tend to be more about what they don't want than what they do. "He left the places, one after another, with the vague sentiment that they were not just what he was looking for. . . . He had never been aware of seeking for anything in particular except when he came to these moments of instinctive rejection."

Abel Teaswith roams from town to town because none are quite right and he doesn't want to become trapped. At one point, in order to get out of a job he doesn't like, he dives off a boat during a storm and nearly drowns. He is certain that there is somewhere better and he has to get there. Like a skittish animal sniffing out a trap, Abel senses when the jaws will close and leaps out of the way. He is listening, watching, testing the ground, and roving until he experiences instinctive rejection's opposite: desire.

There is, in this novel anyway, an end to wandering. When the characters find what they are looking for, they seize it with steely certainty. When Abel meets his future wife, he courts her with "fanatical conviction." They come home for brief periods, comforted the whole time with the knowledge that they will leave again.

Absence, in Wilson's story, is essential to love. The marriage between a sailor and his wife is ideal because they're mostly apart. At one point one of the wives realizes that her husband seems real to her only when he's gone: she's "nearer to him when waiting." Reading this reminded me of the Japanese word *bitai,* which means erotic allure, or getting as close as possible to the object of your affection without actually obtaining it. The word suggests that love is best in the fertile soil of the mind.

Later, when Luella's husband arrives home early, she is disappointed. She realizes that she enjoys waiting—that, though it pains her, waiting's "absence was a form of death." To not wait, to have, is to expect nothing, to be dreamless, desireless, dead. This is one of the dilemmas of marriage: how can you stoke desire for the things you already have? Domesticated love borne out over the years can disappoint with its myriad banalities. The once-prized person fades into the scenery of your life just as a new piece of furniture becomes another object in your living room. The Teaswiths escape this by cycling between separation and reunion. Desire by definition requires not quite having what you want, but the Teaswiths sustain desire even as they're together because they know they will soon be separated. "What makes them worth marrying," Luella's grandmother counsels her, "is the identical thing that has denied so many of them long life in this world." The women love the men precisely because they're always about to leave them.

I wondered to what extent Barbara had internalized her father's worldview. There is no indication that she ever read *No*

More Sea—they still weren't speaking, and I found no mention of it in her writing—but there are scenes in the book that seem explicitly written to her, or to any one of the three daughters he had so far abandoned. Luella adores her father, though she hardly knows him. But she has a consolation: "She kept having in strict secrecy a deep, sweet, womanly premonition that she and her father would one day mean a great deal to each other and be truly close—closer than most parents and children." Wilson might be absent now, but all this would be rectified later.

After her husband's death, Luella decides to thwart her family's fate by running away, inland. She takes her son, Joseph, and moves two thousand miles to Nettleton, a prairie town. Her subversion of the family's destiny ends in disaster. She becomes "unfeminine," "running against the direction of nature." Luella has "a tyrant in her own breast," and that tyrant is love. Love, which makes her a sympathetic character in the beginning, turns her into a monster by the end. She cuts Joseph off from his family and discourages any discussion of the sea. In college, Joseph has a nervous breakdown after hallucinating that a thief was trying to break into his dorm room, and he decides that he can't live anywhere that he can't call out to his mother in the night. She casts out his only worthy lover, a woman strikingly similar to Barbara, who makes the mistake of trying to invite him on a sea voyage. Instead, Luella finds a nice, safe office job for Joseph: a junior partnership at Dowling & Teaswith (a business that Wilson doesn't explain). But the comfortable life is unnatural for him. He carries himself with a droop and his eyes are lifeless. A character says to him, "Joseph: there isn't any you!" Luella's desire to protect her son saps him of all his vibrancy. She realizes that thanks to his nervous breakdown in college, "she had found the way to stultify Joseph's dream for himself without destroying his respect for her." Broken, he would *choose* never to leave her side.

Effectively castrated by his mother, Joseph loses his interest in pursuing women, but Luella wants a grandchild. She selects a pliant schoolteacher who does her the favor of dying in childbirth, but not before she enters a trance and rightly accuses Luella of using her for her womb: "I thought I was going to have a baby of my own once . . . But I was mistaken . . . I do believe he was—yours!"

Luella's plan fails. Her grandson is killed by a tornado while boating on a lake, and Joseph dies trying to save him. Luella brings their bodies back to Penobscot Bay.

No More Sea is so fierce a polemic that it makes one wonder if Wilson was trying to convince the staunchest of all critics: himself. He was getting older. He had no money, no job prospects, and he felt guilty for not being able to send money to Helen and the girls. One day, Margaret sent an anxious letter to friends about his mental health, intimating that he might commit suicide.

He sat at his typewriter near the craggy shoreline insisting that though restlessness is endemic, he was not a callous, roving maniac, but an idealist. He was brave enough, willing to risk enough to find that fount of fulfillment, while everyone else was either too cowardly or unaware to try. But if there was a way to reconcile wandering with family, why hadn't he found it?

At the end of the summer, the vacationers shuttered the colorful cottages that dotted the shoreline and left for their winter homes, but he and Margaret remained. Listening to Margaret's footsteps in the hall, as yet another month passed with no money sent, he must have had flashes of doubt. As he struggled to describe what satisfaction really looks like, he must have felt the inevitable disappointment that every writer feels when the words pale in comparison with the idea in your mind. *No, that's not quite it.* But did Wilson wonder if this feeling was more than just frustration at the ordinary limits of language? Perhaps the confident tone of the book was really the sound of a man straining to drown out the chorus of voices in his head telling him that he would never be satisfied.

Wilson dedicated the book to Margaret. This can be read as a placating gesture. Luella's folly had been to leave Penobscot Bay, and Wilson would not make the same mistake. He may have abandoned his other families, but he would not abandon this one. But from another perspective the dedication can be read as a warning: Don't strangle me with your love. "There is only one way for a woman to get the good of what has been given her. She has got to stand by her menfolk and help them make the best of themselves the way they were born," Luella's grandmother tells her.

No More Sea was published in 1933 to mixed reviews. The *Herald Tribune* praised it but guessed that it wouldn't be widely read. A reviewer from the *New York Times* called the writing "overemotional," the scenes "exaggerated, far-fetched, overdrawn," and lamented that the book "is not at all times convincing."

The book isn't very good, but it proved to be prescient. The parallels between the Teaswiths and the Folletts are obvious, but the family patterns were only just emerging. For now, Wilson's and Barbara's stories were echoing each other. Wilson ran off and then Barbara did. Barbara wrote a book about the call of the wild and then Wilson did. Both father's and daughter's hunger for novelty was insatiable. There was always, surely, a better life somewhere else. The coming years would prove that Wilson had missed the essential lesson of his own book: you cannot run away when the thing you are running from is yourself. The sea is inside you.

SEVEN

We flew to Phuket, in southern Thailand, and took a long wooden boat to an isolated peninsula and jumped off with our luggage into knee-deep turquoise water. We stayed in a bungalow where geckos crept on the woven bamboo walls, and fell asleep over dinner because we were so jet-lagged. In the mornings, we listened to monkeys call to each other in the forest while we drank coffee. After a week, we left for Bangkok on an overnight train, where the American in the seat behind us got a blowjob from a prostitute while we tried to sleep.

We stayed for a while in the spare room of a friend who worked for the foreign service. We immediately got nasty stomach bugs. She kindly vacated her apartment to stay with a friend until the vomiting stopped. Then we moved to a cheap hotel called the Romance Inn. It was located at the end of a long alleyway in a busy part of the city.

"For a cheap hotel, this place has a lot of nice cars in the parking lot," I said to P.J. We hardly ever saw the hotel's other guests, but when we did, they were always beautiful Thai women in skintight dresses. About three days after we arrived, we saw a trio of these women walking down the alleyway arm in arm.

"Are we staying in a brothel?" I asked P.J.

"Yeah, I think so," he said.

I liked the Romance Inn. I wanted to see the entire continuum of Bangkok: everything from the glamorous to the sordid. Of course there was something vampiric about this. Like the johns in business suits who parked their BMWs in the shadowy corners of the parking garage, I too wanted to escape the humdrum of domestic life, to find thrills in foreign places, to get away from the worlds I had known, and to satisfy illicit urges. I could observe, take what I wanted, and leave.

P.J. and I thought that we would stay in Bangkok for a few days and then move on, but those few days quickly turned into forty. When I imagined my ideal city, I saw running trails, lush greenery, bike lanes, and quaint restaurants. Bangkok is a city of more than eight million swarming with people, motorbikes, and cars. Old ladies cook with boiling vats in little carts on sweltering street corners. Sixty-story skyscrapers spike the downtown skyline. The city has 180 shopping malls, between which flashing screens herald the latest fashion. One day, I saw a woman with a disfigured face begging for money in front of a glowing, two-story Christian Dior ad. The city makes little effort to conceal its contradictions, or perhaps it's simply impossible to. Pain and pleasure mingle incomprehensibly. A Buddhist shrine where women dance in traditional makeup can be found down the street from a "massage parlor" where women beckon passing men with a "Hello, handsome." Everywhere we turned there were stands serving ice cream or Chinese bean cakes, street stalls that smelled of tamarind and curry. The next block reeked of sewage. A smiling woman sliced juicy, plump mangoes and placed them on a pearly bed of sticky rice. The sidewalks sizzled and the bank clocks displayed the temperature and the CO_2 levels, which were always extremely high.

A friend's mother who lived in Bangkok invited us to dinner one night. Kerry lived alone in an airy three-bedroom apartment in a posh part of the city, tucked away down a long quiet road. In the grassy courtyard, there were mango trees and sun-bathing cats. She asked where we were staying and we told her about the Romance Inn. "Come stay with me instead," she said, and so we did.

Every morning, P.J. and I would wake up and work for a few hours in our room. Then around midday, we would go for a jog on the track in Lumphini Park, where five-foot-long monitor lizards lurk by the ponds. We would run past the old couples speed walking in matching tracksuits and tourists paddling on the lake in swan-shaped boats. After our run, we would make our way, dripping with sweat, to one of the crowded outdoor lunch markets where young Thai office workers gathered for steaming plates of curried vegetables, meat, fish, and noodles.

At night we often ate in the food courts in one of the malls. At home, we hated shopping malls because they were ours. Part of us wanted the clothes, the furniture, the lives they were selling, and we hated ourselves for being tempted. American malls were monuments to the worst part of the country, the worst parts of us—the parts that are empty, willing to exchange the beauty of the natural world for the comfort of the material world.

But in Bangkok, the malls dazzled us. Their bright bodies lined the major thoroughfares. You could reach them on the Skywalk, which ran beneath the immaculate electric commuter train high above the street. A man in a perfectly white, vaguely nautical uniform and cap saluted us and held open the doors, unleashing a blast of air-conditioning, which was a relief from the city's unrelenting heat. When we stood on the ground floor of one mall and looked up, we saw endless escalators lifting people skyward. The home decor floor was a sea of plush beds, the toy floor a cornucopia of brightly colored Legos, stuffed animals, robots, and playhouses. On the top floor of each mall was a movie theater with enormous ceilings and red velvet carpets. The concession stands sold eight flavors of popcorn. You could get a massage while you watched the latest blockbuster in a recliner in an enormous IMAX theater. We could marvel at Bangkok's malls and at the city itself because the extravagance and inconsistencies weren't ours to judge.

The food courts were crowded with families. We never really knew what we were ordering and paid through a complex food ticket system that we didn't quite understand. The desserts were unrecognizable and we tried them all. One was gelatinous balls that looked like giant fish eyes floating in condensed milk. "What is that?" P.J. asked, poking one of the balls with a fork. "I have no idea," I would say before gulping it down. We rarely liked them but ate them anyway.

Kerry was from the United States but had spent most of her adult life abroad. The three of us became close, cooking together and doing yoga in her living room, having long chats on humid nights while bugs hummed outside. She didn't say so at first, but I sensed there was something painful in her past.

One night, we went around the corner to the Soi 38 night

market, famous for its pad thai and khao soi. Sitting on the crowded street at one of the small outdoor tables next to the food stalls, Kerry told us about the end of her marriage. Her husband had worked in international business. They had lived all over the world, on three continents, working and raising their daughters. But then they moved back to the United States. Not long after, they divorced. The constant moving from country to country had stopped her from seeing that something was amiss. I was anxious to know, was it some vital flaw in the relationship or something that had built up over time? Who had left whom and when had their troubles begun? She didn't seem to know. The divorce was like a large-scale weather event, unpredictable and obliterating. It arrived without warning and left a permanent sense of trauma in its wake. I couldn't tell if this was because of something Kerry wasn't telling us, or if the end of a marriage, generally speaking, doesn't translate to outsiders.

"I never would have imagined it," Kerry said. "We were just like you." I remember thinking, *But you couldn't have been like us because you got divorced.* Sitting across from Kerry, with the curried vegetables congealing on my plate, I dismissed her story because I believed that people who got divorced had inklings all along. *Maybe this won't work out, but I'll give it a shot anyway,* I imagined them thinking. If the ends of other peoples' marriages surprised them, it was because they weren't observant enough. But Kerry was observant. Her husband was a whip-smart businessman, she said. They were, according to Kerry, just like us.

In that first year of marriage, P.J. and I were inseparable. I realized that though I had lived my life constantly surrounded by people at loud dinner tables, in schoolyards, and in classrooms, I had always felt alien on some level, moved by things that did not move others. Until meeting P.J., I had felt cloaked in an otherness that no one seemed to notice. I had close friends but had the impression that some deeper closeness was missing and that it was my fault. But with P.J., my sense of isolation seemed to lift.

One day after running in the park we went to our usual lunch market. It was hot and I felt so sapped of energy I barely ate. I wanted to go back to the apartment, but we were planning a trip to Chiang Mai, in the northern part of the country, and since it was almost the king's birthday, a national holiday, we were concerned that tickets might sell out. We decided P.J. would go to the train station to buy the tickets and I would go home to rest and shower.

As I walked alone from the market to the Skytrain, I looked around at the neatly dressed women in pencil skirts and men in slim business suits. The train's sleek body approached on the monorail. The doors opened and I felt a blast of air-conditioning. An eerily calm recording of a female voice came over the loudspeaker. She seemed to be not so much announcing the next stop as welcoming us to the pinnacle of modernity. "*Nana. Phloen Chit.* Thank you," she said in English and Thai. "Have a nice day." As the train slithered above the sweltering streets, I realized I had not been alone for a single minute in the last month.

P.J. and I went to the grocery store together, worked at a table across from each other, ran together, and at night when we curled up to sleep, I heard him breathing next to me. Without a physical home, P.J. had become my home. Alone on the train, I felt entirely dislocated in ways that were both thrilling and frightening.

Before leaving, we had ambitious plans to travel all over Asia to places as far flung as Indonesia and Nepal. Once we were there, however, our freelance assignments were more sporadic than we had hoped. We needed to be more cautious with our money, so we could only travel to places where the flights were cheap. Nepal and Indonesia were out. We decided to go to Myanmar for a month around Christmas—a cheap forty-minute flight from Bangkok.

Not long after we arrived, I was biking down a dusty road near the reddish-brown temples of Bagan to meet P.J. at a restaurant for lunch, and I got the chills. At the table, I felt a sudden, disconcerting, hollow pang in my stomach followed by more chills, and I knew that I was going to be sick. P.J. asked me with total earnestness, "Do you need a horse cart?" The normalcy and ease with which he suggested it suddenly reminded me of how far from home we were. "Remember our old grocery store?" P.J. would ask me with a laugh in the weeks after my illness. Imagining perusing the aisles with our shopping cart, searching for granola bars, twelve-grain bread, and yogurt was absurd. The lives we used to live seemed a figment to us now, like something we had dreamed up and recalled only vaguely. The time difference made it difficult to keep in touch with our friends and families at home. When we were free in the evenings, they were just starting their workdays and vice versa. We talked to them less and less.

One night we stayed in Taunggyi, the capital of Myanmar's Shan State and headquarters of the Eastern Command of the Tatmadaw, the army. The newspapers said that Myanmar, or Burma as it used to be called, was inching its way toward democracy, and travel books heralded a golden age of travel in the "untouched" country. But there were few signs of this in Taunggyi. As we entered the city by car, we passed vanloads of soldiers holding assault rifles. They stared straight ahead, stone faced, as if looking through us. We passed a large sign that read, "All those who oppose the union will be crushed."

Though we continued to work—by now mostly on freelance assignments for an education blog—we were also tourists, and this fact made us uneasy. We didn't want to be vacationing in a place where the government was engaging in ethnic cleansing in regions of the country where travelers were not allowed. We hoped to justify our presence by volunteering and doing amateur reporting, which of course was a very naïve idea. We contacted a local environmental organization and asked if they needed help with outreach. They said they did. That night we went to dinner at a noodle shop with a woman we met through the NGO. I noticed a group of men at the table next to us with whom the waitstaff seemed particularly preoccupied. The woman recoiled when she noticed one of them. In a hushed tone she told us he was a "businessman," that he owned an airline and was very powerful. She speculated that he was there to meet with government officials, as that was the only thing that could bring him to Taunggyi. "The rules that apply to everyone else," she said, quickly returning to her soup, "do not apply to him." Later she and one of her colleagues would say something disparaging about the Rohingya people who live on the border with Bangladesh. They are stateless, which leaves them vulnerable to drug trade exploitation, human trafficking, and ethnic cleansing. Her shrugging dismissal of the Rohingya left me feeling like I had walked into the wrong bar and found myself sharing drinks with Nazi sympathizers. P.J. and I shot each other furtive glances. Where *were* we?

Outside our hotel window that night, starving gangs of stray dogs barked viciously at each other, occasionally erupting into excruciating yelps. At the end of the month, as we sat in the airport waiting to fly back to Bangkok, we looked out the window and saw fighter jets taking off. I felt relieved but also guilty to be leaving. It had just been a visit, occasionally nightmarish, occasionally beautiful, and it felt extravagant to come and go as we pleased. While we were there, I had been gathering information for an online magazine article I wanted to pitch to an editor I knew, but the piece had fallen apart, and I was glad to be able to drop it. I wasn't sure I wanted to think about Myanmar anymore.

After landing in Bangkok, we went to a fancy dumpling place with our friends who worked for an aid organization. Bangkok is cheap, and though the couple had modest salaries by American standards, they could live in sprawling high-rise apartments and didn't think twice about inviting us to a Michelin-starred restaurant. We had misunderstood the invitation, imagining that the "dumpling place" would be a cheap low-key outing. We arrived in flip-flops and casual clothes; the rest of the clientele was in business attire. Our friends suggested ordering a bunch of dishes to share and we agreed, not wanting to seem cheap or constrain their experience. They proceeded to order what seemed to be the entirety of the menu. "Yes, we'll have two of those. No, make it three." I mentally tallied the bill, each item intensifying the sinking feeling in my stomach. My mind was elsewhere during dinner, and when I looked over at P.J. I knew his was too. The servers were perfectly unobtrusive—invisible and anticipating our every need before we were aware of having it—ferrying out a succession of gorgeously arranged dishes.

After we finished eating, our friends suggested we go see *Life of Pi* in 3-D at one of the mall theaters. There was a fashion show going on in the lobby. When the movie was over, we walked out of the mall into the night air. All around us, the city's electronic billboards flashed in disorienting pulses of light. It was too much. The night had been lavish in a way that felt unjustifiable. I was irritated with our friends for not realizing our financial situation (never mind that we had agreed to everything), but also for how casually they enjoyed the evening's extravagance. As we walked out of the mall, P.J. and I were nearly clinging to each other. The culture shock of our return was far greater than anything we had felt coming from D.C.

Something changed after Myanmar. After a few weeks in Bangkok, we went to Vietnam, and it was there that P.J. realized he didn't want to go to law school. Each acceptance letter that landed at his parents' house gave him an ominous feeling. He suspected he had been motivated to apply by peer and family pressure and the promise (or illusion) of prestige rather than any actual desire to be a lawyer. Now, so far away from home, we began to feel that we could be whatever we wanted, and that if we disappointed friends and family, they would just have to get over it.

P.J. told one school he would not be coming. Then he told another. With each refusal, he seemed lighter. We could go any-where, be anything, and in that breathtaking moment before we chose any one path, we were following them all.

We ran out of money in Laos. Even with our remote work for the education blog, we only had enough for plane tickets back to the United States, and we weren't ready to go back. I had been accepted into a graduate program at New York University based on my proposal to investigate Barbara's life. Class started in the fall, but it was only spring and it seemed unwise to return to the United States penniless and have to wait around for a few months. We contacted our old boss at an American boarding school in Switzerland. We had worked there together the summer after college, teaching English, coaching sports, and organizing activities. It was a ritzy gig—free room and board in a small town with breathtaking mountain views. Best of all, they paid for round-trip airfare. Did they have two last-minute positions for us this summer? They did. We flew back to Bangkok, arranged our visas, and soon were on a plane flying over the Swiss Alps. I'm not sure we stopped long to marvel at the breathtaking ease with which we had been relieved of our financial troubles. It was much easier to wag our fingers at friends than to interrogate our own indulgences.

We flew back to D.C. at the end of the summer to see our families before the move to New York. P.J.'s parents had a barbeque in honor of our return. It was a sunny, late summer day and I was apprehensive about the gathering. In the four months after P.J. made his decision to forgo law school, we had hardly talked to his parents at all. Their reaction had been disbelief, followed by anger, and then an icy silence. Or was the silence ours? It was hard to say who was shunning whom. Now, one wrong word and the barbeque could quickly devolve into anger and resentment. I knew everyone would try very hard not to talk about it, but anticipating all that trying, the not saying, and the forced cheeriness left me feeling depleted before we had even arrived. Driving to the house, I scowled at the neighborhood. Everything suddenly seemed alien to me. The lawns were too manicured. The plants in the gardens were at perfectly measured distances. "When are you moving back?" people asked. *Never,* I thought.

My fear of the looming conflict, my prickly dissatisfaction with everyone and everything around me, made me unable to see that they were asking because they missed us, not out of some desire to control us—though I do think there was a sense that by leaving the family's orbit, we had been led professionally and morally astray. Our travels had somehow both widened our world and constricted it, making people who hadn't experienced the things we had seem impossibly remote from our circle of two. P.J. and I stood on opposite sides of the deck in different conversations.

"What was your favorite part?" someone asked me.

I thought of the time we had been sitting in a coffeehouse in Saigon watching an old man in a wheelchair holding a baby, being pushed by a young woman—three generations strolling down a crowded street. But it seemed like a cliché. Girl goes to Asia, sees people living more vibrantly. *American life = bad. Asian life = good.* The scene of the man in the wheelchair was my idea of people living intimately together—with real connections— when really, that family probably had their own share of misunderstandings. Maybe the old man had berated his son for not going to law school and so they were no longer speaking, and the daughter was forced to care for her father alone, resenting both her father and her brother. I wanted to believe that people in other places had perfected the art of being satisfied, that my disconnection was a problem of geography—not of being human.

I looked over at P.J. and could tell he wasn't really listening to his conversation either. The fact that everything in our lives had suddenly become alien had wrapped P.J. and me more tightly around one another. I thought the distance from our families was a marker of how much we had grown. We had made a fertile little world of our own. We were alone together.

Two days later, we drove a small U-Haul to New York. P.J. found work as an education consultant for an organization with a flexible work schedule. Our lives had an aura of impermanence. We subleased a tiny studio apartment on the Upper West Side and paid our rent in cash at the request of the woman we were subletting from—a person we never saw but who occasionally sent us frantic text messages asking for part of the rent early. The greatest appeal of the arrangement was that it was month to month, and we could leave should something better come up. I would finish my degree, but who knew how long we would stay in New York? I sold our Cuisinart for twenty-five dollars to a man on a bicycle. P.J. left his trombone at a friend's. We told family that we didn't want physical objects for Christmas. We had a single cooking pan because where would we put a second one when we left? We were like people in a hot-air balloon throwing things over the side to make sure we could stay aloft. Knowing that we were light footed, that we could embark at any moment on some unforeseen adventure, was as important as actually going.

Our apartment was so small there was only room for our bed and a small table. The window looked out at a brick wall. When we wanted to know the weather, we had to crouch under the windowsill and crane our necks skyward.

"It's cloudy," P.J. would say, and I would dress for rain.

Sometimes I would jokingly say to P.J., "I'm going into the other room," before walking into the bathroom. The apartment didn't have a fridge so we bought a mini fridge, which we could reach from bed.

While some people professed approval for our wide travel, flexible work schedules, and unencumbered living, it always came with a wink and a nod. "Yes," they said to us, "have your adventures while you can"—meaning, of course, that they would have to end. Whenever I mentioned getting rid of furniture or appliances, people would say, "You'll want those things later." This "later" loomed. Sometime in the near future, circumstances or perhaps people would conspire to trap us. I imagined this threat to my freedom as a large wolf lurking in the bushes waiting to pounce, and felt that if I let my guard down for a moment I would wake up in a house I didn't want, in a neighborhood I didn't want to live in, doing things I didn't want to do. I would sit in my car in traffic and then stare at computers all day in fluorescently lit rooms where the only sounds were the tapping of keyboards and the occasional polite cough. At night I would fold laundry, organize drawers and closets, and pause to wonder when this had become my life.

This threat was a shape-shifter, morphing into whatever anxiety most haunted me at the moment. Sometimes it was a disapproving family; other times it was financial necessity—a medical procedure that would need funding. Sometimes it was a child whose needs, for reasons I couldn't quite imagine, couldn't be met except by moving into the suburbs and working in a job I hated. When I told P.J. about these specters of my future entrapment, none of them sounded quite right. I could not pinpoint what it was that I was really afraid of. On some level I had failed to understand what people were telling me: *you* will want those things. It wasn't that someone was going to force me into a life I didn't want; it was that what I wanted would change. And that was the scariest possibility of all.

EIGHT

In 1931 Barbara and Helen had run out of money. They moved to Manhattan, so Barbara could look for work while Helen finished her book about their sea voyage. Barbara found a job as a secretary at the Personal Research Federation, which analyzed employment trends. She and Helen had rented an apartment in a large brick building in Morningside Heights, overlooking Riverside Park. Sabra finally rejoined them, but the reunion was not what Barbara had imagined. "It was almost a terrible experience, if you want the real truth," Barbara wrote to a friend. "I rushed to her with my heart wide open, and my soul ready for the balm I felt she'd give—and the beautiful dream melted, and I found a little child—a darling little child, to be sure—who took all I could give, and gave almost nothing in return." The sisters seemed baffled by each other. Barbara wrote that Sabra's boundless energy overwhelmed her and Helen, and that "Sabra is rather 'separate.' There aren't many excitements to share, and I guess she finds me a rather dull lump most of the time!" Sabra began to appear less and less in her letters.

Every morning Barbara made her way through the streams of people heading to work and crammed herself onto a subway train headed for Midtown's looming skyscrapers. She sat at a desk all day. At night, she worked on a new novel called *Lost Island* about a girl strikingly similar to herself who, trapped in a job she doesn't like, quits and goes on a sea voyage. Her ship is wrecked and the girl, Jane, lands on an Edenic island with a handsome sailor. Her real life was becoming unbearable to her.

The next summer, Barbara and Helen went on vacation in Vermont. (Sabra, who was seven by then, wasn't mentioned in letters about this vacation. She was likely at summer camp in Lyme, Connecticut.) Barbara by now was seventeen, and she met a group of Dartmouth students, one of whom, Nickerson Rogers, had just graduated. Nick was strikingly handsome with thick, neatly brushed brown hair and the strong build of a quarterback. His slightly hooded dark eyes gave him an intelligent, thoughtful look, and his interest in the outdoors rivaled Barbara's. The group drove up to Maine to hike Mount Katahdin. Barbara and Nick hatched a plan with the others to hike the Appalachian Trail. She was thrilled. The trail was a way out of her life in New York.

Back then the Appalachian Trail was barely a trail at all—it consisted of over 2,000 miles of mostly unmarked wilderness from Mount Katahdin in Maine to Mount Oglethorpe in Georgia. A man named Benton MacKaye had proposed its creation in the early 1920s. He had utopian visions about a place that could "transcend the economic scramble" and be a balm on the American psyche after World War I. He thought the trail could lift people out of the drudgery of modern life. Government workers needed a relaxing place to recuperate, he wrote in his proposal. Housewives, he said, could use the trail's rejuvenating powers too. They could come during their leisure time. It could even be a cure for mental illness, whose sufferers "need acres not medicine." Civilization was weakening, he said. Americans needed a path forward. The Appalachian Trail was the solution.

There was still so much undeveloped land in the United States. The West had Yosemite and Yellowstone, and many more national parks, but the East Coast was the most populous part of the country, and the people who lived there should have something to rival the western parks. National parks already dotted the East Coast's landscape, but what if they could be united? MacKaye imagined what Americans would see as they strode the length of the trail: the "Northwoods" pointed firs on Mount Washington, the placid, pine-rimmed lakes of the Adirondacks. They would cross the Delaware Water Gap, the Potomac, and Harpers Ferry. They could follow Daniel Boone's footsteps through southern Appalachia to the hardwood forests of North Carolina and end at Springer Mountain in Georgia. They would know their country.

Barbara was swept up by the optimism surrounding MacKaye's trail. She covered her bedroom walls with trail maps and wrote excitedly to friends about her plans, sometimes animatedly telling the same person twice. The trail rekindled the ambitious, pioneering spirit that had been simmering while she sat at her desk in Midtown. Large swaths were undeveloped and not yet trodden. Finding her own way was appealing. She wrote to a friend, "Pitting one's strength and personality against the wilds—the greatest sort of opportunity on earth." The trail would harden and refine her. She hoped it would reorient her life.

Two other friends planned to come along. "We're all slightly rebels against civilization," Barbara wrote. "We want to go out into the woods and sweat honestly and shiver honestly and satisfy our souls by looking at the mountains, smelling pine trees, and feeling the sky and the earth." The group met at nearby Bear Mountain to do some preliminary hiking and camping to train for the trip. Knowing she would leave soon made her days at the office drag less. Her life bloomed with possibility. Then the other friends dropped out. Barbara and Nick would go alone.

In July 1932 Barbara quit her job. She walked out of the office for the last time and made her way down the swarming sidewalk, finally free. Her letters from this time are triumphant. She was writing most often to Alice Russell, a thriller writer the Folletts had befriended in Connecticut. She was closer to Barbara's parents' age but was one of Barbara's closest confidantes. "There is always a way out," she wrote to Alice. "There was even a way out of New York."

She couldn't have given up her job at a more inopportune time. New York had a whiff of feral desperation after the stock market crash, and the Depression showed no signs of slowing. A quarter of the U.S. population—nearly thirty million people—was unemployed. Five thousand banks had closed their doors and people had surged in front of the ones that remained open, elbow to elbow, desperate to pull their money out. Beans, noodles, and other cheap foods became staples of the American diet. Meat was done without or saved for Sundays, and whatever scraps were left were thrown into next week's soup. Women patched clothing and traded with neighbors when their children outgrew them.

The recently completed Empire State Building stood empty on Fifth Avenue, as few could afford the rent; people called it "the Empty State Building." A mile away from Barbara's apartment on Riverside Drive, an enormous shantytown was built by the homeless and out of work from scraps of cardboard, crates, and metal. In Lower Manhattan, other shantytowns soon filled the dusty gaps between buildings. Occasionally, the police tried to push people out, but as their numbers grew, the police gave up. At night, the residents covered themselves in old newspapers, trying to keep warm. People waited in lines for hours outside of makeshift kitchens offering watered-down soup. When the soles of their shoes wore out, they lined the insides with cardboard because they couldn't afford leather. When fuel prices got too high, drivers hitched horses to their automobiles, calling them Hoover wagons in a jab at the president.

If Barbara was nervous about quitting her job, she didn't mention it in her letters. She had chosen to eschew security in favor of freedom at a time when many were struggling to survive. She would be traveling alone with a man—scandalous behavior at the time. But Barbara was accustomed to doing as she pleased and didn't put much stock in polite conventions. "I've found this out—you *can't* arrange your life so that everyone is satisfied, including yourself—unless you are a very uninteresting person," she wrote to a friend. If her mother disapproved, it was left unsaid, and she wasn't speaking to her father. When she thought of the future, she tingled with a sense of possibility. There would be woods, sunlight, and fresh air. She would live rough and sleep hard in the cool mountain air. She was awakening while the rest of the world seemed to be cowering.

Barbara and Nick started their journey in Maine. Nick carried a six-pound tent, but often, if the weather held, they unrolled their sleeping bags and slept under the stars. Nick wore shorts, his hiking boots, no shirt, and a red kerchief around his neck. It wasn't long before he was getting tan and strong. He stopped shaving. As the months passed, his beard reminded her of something out of a Russian novel. "You can't kill his looks," Barbara wrote a friend. She wore dungaree pants and a blue shirt. Her muscles became defined again. She felt her body reawakening after her time in the city. Nick cut her hair short and sometimes people on the trail mistook her for a boy, but she didn't mind. In fact, she seemed to relish it.

In October, they took shelter at the Moosilauke Summit Camp in New Hampshire's White Mountains. They stayed in the same winter cabin Barbara had once stayed in with her father. Frost feathers—delicate ice formations—spread over the windows. Some were six inches long. They were exquisite, all the more so because they couldn't last.

Barbara wrote a letter to her father from the winter cabin. She had no idea where he was, so she enclosed it in a letter to Alice. She doubted it would ever reach him and left instructions for Alice to destroy it if he couldn't be found.

Somewhere along the trail, Barbara and Nick became lovers. Barbara had been dating someone else, a sailor named Anderson, whom she had met during the Caribbean and South Seas voyage. She wrote him a letter breaking it off. She was sorry to have to do it, especially as Anderson continued to profess his love for her, but he was too often at sea. They hadn't seen each other in months. She was living a mountain life now and all her energy was focused on Nick. She wrote to her mother, "We haven't even scrapped at all, which is rather remarkable, considering how constantly and intimately we've been together since July. I've never had such an enjoyable and satisfactory relation with anyone."

"God knows I may end up in an awful mess," she wrote to Alice. "Still, all I can do is follow the best I know—take the greenest and most verdurous trail that I can see. If it ends in a desert or a swamp, maybe I can go back and try another one. And that makes a cosmic adventure of it all." Life was not something to be handled delicately. Intoxicated by what she had done, she wrote, "I've jumped the whole structure of what life was before: I've jumped the job, jumped my love, jumped parental dependence, jumped civilization—made a pretty clean break— and am happier than for years and years. I've a new, and I think better, structure of life, though time alone can tell that!"

Inviting chaos into your life—quitting your job, leaving your family, breaking up with your boyfriend—can be a clarifying tonic. In a state of upheaval the minor concerns of daily living are summarily dismissed. But it is also terrifying, if you allow yourself to pause and think about it.

The trail was difficult. Since it was uncut, they had to make their way using rough maps and following bends in rivers. Some days the mist was so thick they couldn't see more than a few feet in front of them. They bought a canoe for twenty dollars and paddled across lakes and rivers so choppy that Barbara was surprised the canoe wasn't smashed to splinters.

She wanted to wear herself out. Before she left for the Appalachian Trail, she wrote, "There will be times when we'll probably be cold and wet and uncomfortable and grumpy. But we're ready for that—almost covet it in fact." She couldn't climb the Appalachian Trail, she couldn't write novels, she couldn't have an epic, adventurous relationship and personal revolutions if she wasn't willing to sweat.

Barbara and Nick crossed the mossy woods that ran along streams in the Presidential Mountain range. She felt herself transforming. "I'm healthier, browner, stronger, and happier than for years; it is the swellest kind of life: all out of doors, warm and cold, wet and dry, sunshine and moonlight, fir boughs and sleep from sunset till dawn; lakes and rivers and hills, trails and wild country and long white roads." They swam in lakes and panned for gold. They didn't seem to mind when they didn't find any. They didn't need much and what they did could fit on their backs. The way they were living before seemed so timid and encumbered now. "God! what a lot of junk civilization involves," Barbara wrote. This was the person she was supposed to be. The life she wanted was coming into view.

As winter approached, the trail got too cold and they decided to end their journey near the Massachusetts border, six hundred miles from where they had started. She returned briefly to her mother's apartment and then met Nick in Massachusetts.

They hit the road again a couple of weeks later, this time aboard the S.S. *Rex* heading from New York to Gibraltar. They eventually settled in Mallorca. Barbara learned Spanish and ran hard on the Mediterranean beaches in her bathing suit beside a jet-black wolfhound that belonged to a Spanish soldier. To make money they worked in a pension run by two Englishwomen. Barbara swept rooms, peeled potatoes, and washed dishes while Nick polished shoes, lit fires, chopped wood, and served in the restaurant. Barbara despised the women who ran the pension, but it didn't matter because she was having such a good time with Nick. At night, they drank muscatel and sherry in cafés and went dancing.

They were "poor as church mice," as she put it. She still wasn't speaking to her father. She wrote disparagingly of him but also admitted, "I do want to look him up again sometime." As for her plans, she had several exciting schemes. "We shall probably establish ourselves in a shack in the woods somewhere and explore from it. I like civilization less and less." At one point Barbara tried to get a copyediting job at a publishing house in Germany. The future seemed promising and full of action.

For the sake of propriety, they pretended to be married. Nick introduced Barbara with total ease as Mrs. Rogers, which delighted her. The girl who had been so sure that she never wanted to be married was now having quite a lot of fun playing wife. Barbara grew more freckled and Nick loved the little brown spots, calling them "out of doorsy." He told her she was beautiful, which made her feel beautiful. This was better than marriage—something in between.

To her mother she wrote, "You have no idea how much fun it is to be married. I mean, when you really aren't." Helen was divorced and still living with Sabra in New York. Barbara was distancing herself from what she saw as her mother's mistakes. She was toying with the idea of marriage, dancing around it, trying to fit the pleasurable parts of commitment into her independence and leaving out the baggage. In the same letter, she wrote, "We have agreed that the first requisite of a happy marriage is not to be married." It was like a Zen koan.

On Saturday, July 7, 1934, when Barbara was twenty, they did get married. Maybe they grew tired of pretending. Or maybe marriage felt like another adventure. There are no letters from this time. They had returned to the United States and settled in

Brookline, Massachusetts—no shack in the woods and no publishing job. Nick had a burgeoning interest in photography and eventually got a job with Polaroid as an engineer. Barbara found work as a secretary and continued to work on *Lost Island*. For the first time, their lives were relatively still.

NINE

During our second winter in New York, P.J. and I moved from the Upper West Side to Brooklyn. We settled into a routine, working reasonable hours, mostly from home—P.J. at one end of our breakfast table, I at the other. Our window overlooked a street where we could see men delivering boxes to the delis, the clothing store, or the pharmacy across the street. Children ran down the sidewalks on their way to and from the primary school around the corner, and construction workers climbed the scaffolding on the church next door. We jogged every other day, usually through Prospect Park. First we would pass the vast Long Meadow, then the baseball fields, then the lake, followed by a stretch of woods, eventually arriving where we had started at Grand Army Plaza. Some days we ran through the park in the opposite direction to change things up. We went out to dinner or bars a few nights a week with friends. Other nights we read or watched movies or TV shows. On Sundays, we picked up the newspaper, and if it was warm enough, we brought coffee to the picnic tables in the little park around the corner from our apartment and read. Everything was in walking distance. Everything was a slight variation on what we had done the week before. Weeks turned into months.

One Sunday, sitting in the little park, I came across an article written by the novelist and city wanderer Teju Cole. He was traveling through Switzerland, photographing the snowy peaks of the mountains and the neat little public squares. He wrote about *heimweh,* a Swiss German word for homesickness, which, as legend has it, was coined by Swiss mercenaries who "missed home with a deranging intensity, longing for the high elevation of their cantons, their clear lakes, their protective peaks." *Heimweh,* Cole explained, had an antonym: *fernweh,* a longing for far-off places, "is similar to wanderlust but, like *heimweh,* has a sickish, melancholy tinge."

I looked around me at the people in the park. They all looked like us. They were thirtysomething couples wearing casual-chic clothes befitting young Brooklyn professionals relaxing on the weekend. Many had French bulldogs or terriers, sleek strollers, or shopping bags. I looked at P.J. reading the paper across from me. I looked at our clothes and matching coffee cups and thought back to the time right after we had returned from Asia. I remembered not wanting to eat in restaurants. It had seemed an expensive way to fill some void that was more than a hunger for food. Every time I started a new movie, bought something, or went out to dinner, I had the sense that these diversions were hollow, that I was just filling the time until the end of something—and that something was my life.

The decisions I made—this or that coffee, this or that movie, this or that dentist—were meaningless, yet my life was packed to the brim with these inconsequential microdecisions that all related to entertaining or taking care of myself. I seemed to live on the surface of the world rather than in it. And perhaps most troublingly of all, dealing with this sensation didn't feel urgent. I saw the ways in which I could continue like this forever—how, on some level, I might want to.

Part of me wanted to stay in our apartment. Part of me cherished our routine. Part of me found the idea of leaving again, of getting on a plane and going somewhere new frightening. I had traveled all over the world, lived on three continents, and foreign places still conjured the specter of danger: machetes at night, rusty nails, the covetous eyes of thieves, humid hospital rooms with mosquito netting. Part of me preferred our neighborhood and our routine because those things were safe.

But I didn't like that part of myself. Occasionally, I had a daydream about having a conversation with an elderly me. In the daydream, old me is propped up by pillows on her deathbed, a white comforter draped over her lap. Her hair is long and white, arranged in a bun on the top of her head. She points her gnarled old-lady finger at me. "You weren't brave enough," she says with withering finality. "You got one chance, and you blew it." Her words and dismissive demeanor sting. She is right. I am scared and awfully tempted to pursue only comfort.

I considered the idea that I was at another turning point, that now my life was operating on a fairly predictable cycle in which every couple of years I was faced with a decision: stay or go. I could ignore the itch for something new, continue with things the way they were, or I could make a drastic change. The possible lives that would result from those two options were very different, and this excited and scared me—it excited me because, at nearly thirty, the facts of my life were still malleable. It scared me perhaps for the very same reason.

Helen's book about her sailing voyage with Barbara was called *Stars to Steer By*. The book ends at a dock in Gray's Harbor, near

Hoquiam, Washington. The five-masted, two-hundred-foot *Vigilant* they had sailed in on was moored. They stood on its deck alone. All of a sudden, Barbara announced that she wanted to climb the rigging and sit on the crosstrees—the T-shaped wooden beams at the topmast, over one hundred feet in the air. When she reached the top, she stood suspended above the decks, the harbor, and the other ships. In the distance, she could see the evergreen hills of pine, fir, and spruce. She thought about a Tongan prince who had proposed to her during the voyage, but that thought was soon eclipsed by another: the sea. Why would she marry a Tongan prince when she could have the whole world? They were only just to shore and she felt a fierce hunger to set sail again. Helen ends the book with the question Barbara always asked when they were on land too long: "When do we go to sea again?"

One night, between Honolulu and Washington, Helen and Barbara stood on the deck. Clouds sped across the night sky in front of the moon. "Everything was racing," Helen wrote, "sea, moon, clouds, ship."

"On like this forever and ever . . . ," Barbara said, feeling the thrust of the ship, the wind against her face and through her hair.

Helen turned to Barbara and asked, "Are you satisfied now, shipmate? Have you everything?"

"Everything," Barbara said. "It's perfect."

She wanted *everything*. In her novels, she imagines that satisfaction can be found in a place. But we don't see the place in *The House Without Windows*. In *Lost Island,* Barbara is dishonest about what could really satisfy her protagonist. Jane was a thinly veiled version of herself, and she never would have been content to stay on any one island forever. But that moment on the deck of the *Vigilant,* as she stood in the dark, heading off to a new adventure, Barbara had finally found what she was looking for. She wanted motion. There was no single place for Barbara, no single life. She wanted all the places so she could be endlessly stirred by wonder.

Wanting everything seems like an excellent way to set yourself up for disappointment. But what if you accept the yearning, what if the yearning is the only thing that can satisfy? Wilson had sought to describe this idea in *No More Sea,* settling on a hunger for perpetual motion between land and sea.

Teju Cole wrote of *fernweh,* "The cure and the disease are one and the same." Once you satisfy the need to be in the faraway place by going there, the place is no longer far away. It is like the horizon—a place you can never reach. What you need is a vessel—something to transport you, push you onward to the next island and the next and the next.

What went wrong with Barbara and Nick depends on whom you ask. I found a record of their divorce papers in the archives at Columbia University. It lists Barbara's absence as the reason for the divorce. She had, at that point, been missing for three years. I had always found this length of time surprising, mostly because Nick had actually wanted a divorce months before Barbara vanished, so waiting three years seemed like a long time, though perhaps it was understandable under the circumstances. But one day, while searching another newspaper archive, I found an article showing that he had, in fact, tried to divorce Barbara once before, two years after she vanished. Barbara's family, as far as I could tell, did not know about this divorce attempt. I quickly contacted the Middlesex Probate Court and requested the documents. A few weeks later, they came in the mail. They were different from those he filed the second time, most notably for the reasons he stated for wanting a divorce. They neglected to mention the fact that, at this point, no one had seen Barbara in two years.

December 12, 1941, the day Nick testified at the Middlesex Probate and Family Court in Cambridge, Massachusetts, was one of the coldest days of the year. He told the judge that Barbara had been "cruel" to him. His examples were that she had vetoed his suggestions for entertaining guests at a party, "failed to cooperate at home," and went on summer vacation without him. The judge, John C. Leggat, interrupted.

"Did she ever strike you? Are you afraid of her?" he asked.

"No," Nick said.

"Did she take care of the home?"

"No," Nick answered, adding that it was he who had installed their curtains—not she.

"That is no cause for divorce," Judge Leggat said. He dismissed the case.

Reading these documents recalled the passage in *The House Without Windows* when Eepersip comes across a little cottage in the woods and is momentarily entranced. But she snaps out of it and sees "those useless decorations called curtains. To think of it! when there was a carpet so much lovelier of green grass or of white sand—and no windows to be curtained!" It was an uncanny detail, a coincidence, but it showed that Barbara had been prescient, had imagined as a twelve-year-old child that houses would be snares for her. But were housekeeping details really what ended the marriage?

The year before Barbara vanished, Nick was traveling often with Edwin Land, a cofounder of Polaroid, experimenting in polarizing light for photography. Barbara was working at the American Board for Commissioners for Foreign Missions, a Christian missionary society, as a secretary. The offices were on Beacon Street, just around the corner from their apartment; her daily comings and goings had contracted to a few blocks. She had only recently started speaking to her father again and had not published a book since the age of fourteen, though she continued to write regularly.

She had spent five years, off and on, working on *Lost Island,* but those days were over. She had hoped to sell it to Harper & Brothers, but they didn't take it.

Thanks to Nick's job, they had financial stability. Barbara's family had never been fiscally savvy, mostly because they weren't very interested in money. The security Nick's job provided seemed to have a flattening effect on her. Without something to struggle for, she was reminded of what she was missing. She wrote to Alice, "My greatest worry now, when I have time to stop and think about it, is that I am in a rather difficult position as far as Adventure is concerned where that evasive spirit may have trouble locating me! Life right now is a very *quiet* adventure, though pleasant, at that."

She was studying dance and growing weary of her work. "I am at the same job, doing much the same things as before, and liking it just well enough to hang on; or, rather, not disliking it quite enough to leave." She had a vague sense that something more to her liking was out there. "If I had any bright ideas about what to leave it *for* I might actually leave," she wrote, but she couldn't muster the urgency she had once felt. The world seemed to be constricting—the adventures on ships, the dramatic mountain scenery, the long, action-filled days spent discovering new wooded paths seemed so distant to her now.

In the summer of 1938, she and Nick couldn't get coinciding vacation time from work, so they spent much of the summer apart. Or at least that's how Barbara told it. In letters she makes it sound like an unfortunate but unavoidable matter of mismatched work calendars. She doesn't mention that Nick was upset. But this was the summer that Nick cited in his divorce papers—when Barbara went on vacation without him.

Barbara was given a month off from work. She went on a canoe trip in Canada with a friend. She was in touch with her father again, so she visited him, Margaret, and their two children for a week in Bradford, Vermont. Wilson and Margaret's daughter, Jane, was three, and their son, Wilson Tingley, whom they called "Ting," had just been born. They were living in a house overlooking the Connecticut River "with not an ugly thing in sight," as her father liked to say. Margaret and Wilson had been married for four years, and Margaret and Barbara were on good enough terms to now regularly write letters to each other, though the letters no longer exist. Barbara and her father spent an afternoon gardening together. She described that day as "heavenly," though she still remarked, "I can never really be myself with them, they are so sort of formal without at all meaning to be." Wilson and Margaret were in extreme financial distress—they were at risk of being evicted from their home—but Barbara noted that their children were thriving, and she mostly recalled the visit fondly.

The next summer, the summer of 1939, she went on vacation alone again. Nick was traveling all across the country for work. Barbara visited Alice and her friend Marjorie Houser Susie in California. (Marjorie was a close but relatively recent friend of Barbara's, though little is known about their relationship since their letters no longer exist.) While in California, Barbara also attended a dance program. Modern dance was her new obsession and she took classes with "big shots" at Mills College, in Oakland. She had planned a longer stay with Alice, but while she was there, a letter arrived from Nick. The marriage was over, he said.

Barbara was stunned. There had been no warning—or at least so she claimed. She handed the letter to Alice and Marjorie and they pored over it, trying to understand. The wording was vague, but something in it—or perhaps the suddenness of the decision—made the women think that Nick was having an affair. Barbara didn't know it at the time, but Nick was so certain of his decision that he sent an identical copy of the letter to Bennington, Vermont, her stop prior to California, in case she was still there.

Barbara got on the next bus to Brookline. The trip took five days and she hardly slept. The broad flat expanse of the golden prairies rolled by her window, but she didn't notice it. Instead she imagined scenes from the conversation she would have with Nick, rehashing the things she would say to him, the things he might say to her. She thought about the possibility of another woman. Who was she—if she even existed? If Nick was leaving her for another woman, then history was on repeat. Her marriage was ending exactly as her parents' had. She was determined not to let this happen. They would work through it.

Maybe she shouldn't bring up the possibility of another woman, she thought. In her letters to Alice from this time, she argued that she was to blame, not him—though how exactly she didn't say. Marriages fall apart in pieces—each wrong and misunderstanding, small on its own, adding to the weight of a pile. Nick had declared their pile insurmountable, but Barbara was sure he had acted too soon. She just needed to convince him. She saw saving her marriage as a question of strategy. If she just thought about it enough and behaved intelligently, she could change his mind. It doesn't seem to have occurred to her that feelings are more unruly than that. She sent Alice a postcard from Kansas City. "Am really feeling O.K. and well under control!" She thanked her for all her moral support and said she would write as soon as she had news. She was scared but hopeful.

Barbara was shaking when she finally arrived at the apartment on Tuesday night. But when she opened the front door, it was dark and still. No one was home. This was better, she told herself; Nick's absence would give her a chance to take a bath and rest. But as she walked through the rooms, she noticed that Nick's toothbrush was missing. So was a piece of luggage. She panicked, lunging at the phone, dialing every number she could think of. Nobody answered.

Finally she reached someone at Polaroid. She told the man on the other end of the line that she had come home unexpectedly from vacation and needed to speak to Nick immediately. Nick was in New York, the man said, but would probably be back in Brookline the next day. He told her the name of a hotel where he might be staying. Barbara called the hotel, but Nick wasn't there.

She got on the phone again and this time she reached a doctor friend. He came right over with sleeping pills, whiskey, and hamburgers. He told her she was lucky that Nick wasn't home that night, that it would be better to see him when she was more in command of her emotions.

In the morning, the world seemed a shade different. The apartment now appeared well lit and alive with the sounds of passing cars and people from the street below. The frenzy had released her, and in its place was a weary calm. She spent the day quietly tidying up the apartment, reading, and listening to the radio. The coal-fire engine on the B&A Railroad that ran down her street occasionally rumbled by. She didn't leave the house, waiting for the phone to ring with some news of Nick.

The phone did ring at least twice that day, but it wasn't Nick. One time it was someone from Polaroid, and the next time it was Nick's younger brother, Howard. He said he would come for dinner to keep her company and Nick would probably return that night. But Nick didn't come home that night or the next. Barbara couldn't recall how she spent the time; all the waiting and worrying seemed to obliterate the present.

Nick finally appeared on Friday. He told Barbara that yes, he was having an affair, though he didn't tell her if it was serious or whom it was with. Barbara dug her nails into her hands and listened. She didn't say anything reproachful. "I don't blame him in the least," she wrote to Alice. "He really thought I didn't care; only, instead of saying anything about it so that I could have done something about it before, he just kept quiet and everything slid and slid. But it's really my fault; I had it coming to me, I know . . . I think that, if I can really prove that I'm different, why maybe things will work out." It was she who needed to change, she believed, not him. She thought of her mother. She would not wind up like her—left by her husband for another woman. "I think maybe I could teach Helen a thing or two or three at this point!" she wrote to Alice. "I wonder if maybe she could not have won her game, if she had played it cautiously and quietly."

Immediately after Nick's return, they went to Vermont and then to Cape Cod because they had long-standing plans to do so. They swam and sailed with their friends and tried to snatch moments alone to discuss their "Situation," as Barbara called it. It must have been awful, to play the happy couple frolicking in the sun but to know all the time that the marriage might be over. In Cape Cod, Barbara asked Nick if he wanted to save the relationship. It's strange that she allowed ten days to pass before asking this, but guessing at feelings and motives was her method rather than frank conversation. And Barbara knew she might not like the answer. "I had had the feeling up till then that he definitely did not want to," she wrote to Alice. "So imagine my amazement, my almost hysterical delight, when he said yes, he wanted to make a go of it. Right away he qualified it, of course."

"Don't get too excited about that," he told her. "I'm not sure that I can." Barbara was thrilled, despite his cautioning. If he wanted to, that was all she needed. She would be on her best behavior. She would win him back. When they got back from Cape Cod, for reasons that her letters don't explain, they began to look for a new apartment. Nick told Barbara she could do the hunting, which she took to be a promising sign.

During this time, Marjorie counseled Barbara closely. Marjorie had been with her in California when Nick's letter arrived and Barbara relied on her input. At one point, Marjorie even telephoned Nick to discuss their problems with him and reported the conversation back to Barbara. It's a telling detail: Barbara didn't feel she could talk to Nick directly.

Barbara became a sleuth of sorts, trying to figure out what had gone wrong in order to save the marriage. Some days she felt quite hopeful. Others, she thought divorce was imminent. Nick was the laconic type so she had to look beyond his words for clues. "This morning, when he left to go to work, he gave me a sort of rough pat which is absolutely the first gesture of affection of any kind that has come my way!" she wrote at the end of August. She watched him when he came home from work. She thought she detected a small change in his demeanor. "He *looks* a little different, more natural, less strained. He *moves* more in the old easy manner—not harshly, abruptly, angrily, as at first. And he *sounds* different . . . the tortured note, and the tortured look, the terrible strain, the angry glowering, have pretty much disappeared."

Another sign: he encouraged her to quit her job to find a more rewarding one. "He wants to see me live about as fully as possible," she wrote. At first this concern for her well-being struck her as a good omen. But then a dark thought occurred to her. Housework—and her unwillingness to do it—had been central to their disagreements. If she had a new, more demanding and interesting job, she would presumably do less housework. "It apparently doesn't mean as much to him as I thought it did, to have me personally doing it." Now she was confused. If housekeeping was not where she had gone wrong, then what was it? She considered the idea that he was encouraging her to find a better job so that he could feel less guilty about leaving her. She hadn't been feeling like herself. Even her dancing had changed. "I get tired terribly easily, and am afraid I've lost a lot of what I gained this summer in strength and ability." She wasn't sleeping. And Nick must have noticed the anxious way she read his every movement. "I feel that maybe the holes into which I fell are still uncharted after all!"

She was right. One hole in particular was still uncharted, but she refused to look there: Nick's affair. What kind of pull was this new love exerting on him? "I have no way of knowing," Barbara wrote. "Nick is the kind of person who may very well *never* tell me just what it was all about." She didn't know if the relationship was serious, how long it had been going on, or even if it was still going on. And, perhaps most tellingly, she didn't ask. Perhaps Nick would have told her but she didn't really want to know. The threat of someone else was too great—and too far beyond her control. Like a foreign species entering the delicate ecosystem of their marriage, the lover could wildly alter the environment.

Working through their problems was "going to be a long, slow job—almost intolerably so," Barbara wrote. But chipping his way through the plaque of marital resentment likely didn't sound very appealing to Nick, who was probably comparing that relationship to the clean slate he had with the other woman. It could take years with Barbara—if it ever happened at all. Nick was keeping a running tab of Barbara's wrongdoings, and the smallness of some of the complaints suggests that he was looking for reasons to leave. Barbara could do a better job of taking care of the house, she could be more attentive, but she could not make Nick fall out of love.

"I think I am getting to be quite a woman of iron and steel," she wrote to Alice in late August. "I think I've persuaded him to give me my chance . . . I think I'll get it, and I think I can win if I've got the strength. I think he is a steady enough person, and a kind enough person and also enough of an easy-going person, so that he won't go making drastic plunges if he doesn't have to; and if I can make a pleasant sort of life for him, I think he'll hang on." *I think, I think, I think.*

At night, she took sleeping pills. "The days I can stand, because they are sort of full of little things; but the nights I could never stand without some kind of help in achieving oblivion!" She had envisioned herself as a brave adventurer. She was the one who left. But now, for the second time, the most important person in her life was on the verge of leaving her behind. The cycle was beginning again and she knew it. In November came her most ominous letter yet, written to Alice:

In my last letter I told you things were going well, and I thought they were. They continued to go well for a time—at least I thought so, and I was happy, and decided that the worst part of the ordeal was over. But that was too easy. No such luck! I don't know what to say now. On the surface things are terribly, terribly calm, and wrong—just as wrong as they can be. I am trying—we are both trying. I still think there is a chance that the outcome will be a happy one; but I would have to think that anyway, in order to live; so you can draw any conclusions you like from that!

By December she was gone.

ELEVEN

It took Nick two weeks to report his wife's disappearance. Around 10:00 P.M. on December 21, 1939, he walked out of their apartment and into the Brookline police station, an imposing building with large, arched windows and a manicured lawn. He approached the reception desk and told the officer he was there to report a missing person. The policeman recorded his statement in a black leather-bound logbook. Nick went to the morgue on Charles Street too, but he didn't find Barbara there.

Then he waited some more. Barbara missed Christmas, the New Year, and her birthday in March. Later that month, he moved a few miles away to Cambridge and went back to the police station to give his new address in case anything turned up. In April, he went back again. This time, the police released an eight-state bulletin. Nick gave a more detailed description, which the officer took down in neat, black script:

Missing from Brookline since Dec. 7, 1939. Barbara Rogers, married, Age 26, 5-7, 125, fair complexion, black eyebrows, brown eyes. Dark auburn hair worn in a long bob, left shoulder slightly higher than right. Occasionally wears horn rimmed glasses.

No one responded to the bulletin. Nothing was written in the paper. No real investigation began.

When you walk out on someone it pauses the lives of those left behind. The vanished person's clothes still hang in the closet, their books still rest on the nightstand, their mail continues to arrive. A long brown hair on Barbara's pillow could have reminded Nick that she had only just been there. She was gone, but not entirely.

It is not clear if Barbara's parents knew right away that she was gone. Nick must have told them by Christmas, when it would have been strange not to hear from her. When Helen found out, she largely left the details of the investigation up to Nick. He told her that the police in both Brookline and Boston were handling the case and that he would let her know if he heard anything. She was struggling with arthritis and vision issues, and she would later say that she didn't get involved actively in the search because she was busy raising Sabra, who was now in high school. Besides, she trusted Nick to handle it. None of Helen's letters or diaries from the time immediately following Barbara's disappearance survive, so we can only speculate about her thinking.

Wilson didn't seem to feel he was in a position to intervene. He had seen Barbara and Nick very little over the years and had never been comfortable around Barbara's husband. Nick was quiet and unpretentious, while Wilson was literary and formal. They were awkwardly at odds.

At first, both Helen and Wilson expected Barbara to return. She had taken off before without notice or explanation, and so they reasoned that perhaps for the time being she did not wish to be found. While they had to admit that something terrible could have happened, they clung to more optimistic theories. Helen imagined that she had gone to sea. Wilson speculated that she had created an entirely new identity somewhere else. But as time passed, these scenarios seemed increasingly unlikely, and more sinister thoughts began to plague them. Helen considered the possibility that Barbara was lying in a hospital somewhere, suffering from amnesia or a nervous breakdown. What if she were dead? What if she had been murdered? Still they did nothing.

A year after Barbara went missing, Wilson heard a car coming down his drive as he was shoveling snow from his walkway in Vermont. It was freezing, just after dusk, and the car got stuck in the snow. He put down his shovel and didn't think much of it until he heard a female voice call out. His heart skipped a beat. It was Barbara. In a moment he would have her in his arms. He ran over to the car, calling out, "Hullo! Hullo, there!"

But of course it wasn't Barbara. It was just a young woman trying to find a shop to repair her typewriter. A phantom Barbara. His spirits plunged. But his disappointment transformed into hope. His certainty that it *could* have been Barbara had revealed something important to him.

In May 1941, a year and a half after Barbara vanished, Wilson published an anonymous letter in the *Atlantic*. It's addressed to Barbara. He began by explaining that he could not believe she had been gone for a year: "It is preposterous that such a one should just drop out of existence for that length of time, as if she were one of the indistinguishable crowd." He tells her about the woman with the typewriter: "Up to that evening, cold reason had made me partly doubt myself. Others to whom I should have looked for equal or greater faith had said that you were surely dead. When I told them steadily that you were surely not, did I quite believe my own words, or was I silencing with protest a conviction in my own mind that these others must be right—a certitude more dreadful than I could muster the courage to face quite yet?" But the woman had shown him what he truly believed: "It was brought home to me in February a few weeks after you vanished how deep, instinctive, and unshakable is my faith that you live and remember and in your own time will let us know how you fare. . . . I knew that you are you, that you would come."

"I have seen you at best, for only a few days of any year, a few hours of any day. Yet then, as in the long interval and always, you were one of the permanently important persons in your father's cosmos—the cosmos, you will at least grant, of someone to whom the few human beings who are necessary are very deeply necessary. What would it mean to the dweller in a mountain valley if a peak that he had contemplated steadily for a quarter of a century were suddenly blotted from the landscape? I do not have to tell you, to whom everything above the timber line is both thrilling and familiar."

Wilson was now living in the myopia of family he had sought to avoid. The world was at war. The radio brought news of the Blitz and Hitler's order for the invasion of the Soviet Union. Plans were already under way for Japan's attack on Pearl Harbor. But Wilson, who typically followed the news closely, suddenly didn't care. "I say to myself in the morning, 'This may be the very day when she will come, or word from her or of her,' and it seems that the sun is riveted *in situ,* that the hour for the mail stage will never arrive, that the moments are not successive drops in the flow called time, but each a frozen eternity."

Barbara's disappearance was a stunning reversal of the plot Wilson had imagined in *No More Sea.* In the book, the women lived their lives on the near end of a telescope, staring out to sea, waiting for men who would never come home. But now Wilson was the one who waited. He was learning that waiting for someone you love, when you're not sure they will return, is agony.

He looked out his kitchen window on the cornfield behind his house, standing where Barbara had stood just a couple of years before when she had declared the garden too weedy. They had spent the day side by side, sweating as they pulled weeds out of the patch. The "eternal Now," the wonderful feeling of total absorption in the present moment, had been destroyed by a "crawling agony of suspense." He came across a book he thought Barbara might like and set it aside for her. When she came back, she might want to read it.

Wilson's letter to the *Atlantic* seemed to take for granted that she had run away:

> I think you launched your one-woman strike against a system of deferred payments and for the right to live richly, fully, fulfillingly in the continuous present.
>
> It would profoundly interest me—I say it in admiration and love, without ironic intention—to know this: Have you found that right so simply obtainable? Or are you perhaps still assuring yourself that life will soon begin to assume the shape of your demands?—as soon, say, as you have recovered from the unavoidable wrench of separation, ceased to be hounded by a feeling that you are a deserter, and created for yourself a new place, a new identity?

He is shaming her, but there is a trace of envy in his tone—she had done what he had tried to do—and also of guilt. After the divorce, he had wanted to create a new life. He began a new family with Margaret. They had three children. He almost completely lost touch with the children from his previous marriages. He had even gone so far as to change his name. Roy was what Helen had called him. He had gone by Wilson (his middle name) professionally, but after the divorce he started using Wilson in all areas of his life. Margaret called him Wilson. Their children together thought of him as Wilson. In a new name, there is the wish for a new life—and the belief that we *can* start fresh if we make some gesture of demarcation.

In his letter, Wilson pleads with Barbara to understand the pain she is causing him, "Surely you will not recoil from knowing just this: that simply, humanly, sorely, I miss you." He admonishes her, "To pretend that one could freely loop back, begin over, reverse oneself, be born again—that was to decimate, not to fulfill, oneself . . . life being so short and we not granted the option of trying its imperfect passages over again."

Wilson repeated the refrain of his novel: "a normal woman cannot be herself without giving herself. Whatever she holds back, on some theory of saving her independence, her freedom of initiative, her selfhood, she holds back first of all from herself. There are two-person relationships—parenthood, marriage, all friendship worth the name—that by their very nature constantly ask you to throw yourself wholeheartedly into serving the other person's necessities." But Barbara was not like the Teaswith women. She was more like the Teaswith men.

In 1947, eight years after Barbara vanished, Helen also wrote to her. It was an anguished poem that slips uncomfortably between her dueling beliefs that Barbara was alive and that she wasn't:

Where are you, child of the mountains and of the sea?
Did you climb the heights
To reach for the sun?
Did you sail over the horizon
To touch a lonely star?
You who created for all of us a shining world
of freedom and of radiance in words of
startling beauty,
Did you try to find that land?
Did you yearn for its beauty, its freedom?

'Tis well for you, my precious one. But for me, your
    mother?
You left me chained to fear and awful imaginings,
To a constant searching on
Buses, street cars, subways, trains, ships, planes—for
Your face among the millions,
The deep brown eyes, the hair, copper-tinted in
    the sun,
the puckish nose and laughing mouth,
You left me chained to despair and to a fading hope.
Come back, child of the mountains and of the sea!

Three years after Barbara vanished, Nick's request for a divorce was finalized. He married Anne Bradley, the woman he'd had the affair with, though the affair was never mentioned in the divorce proceedings. Both times he filed, he said Barbara was at fault. She hadn't taken care of the house. She had deserted him.

It's not clear what year Anne met Nick, or under what circumstances. Another journalist who interviewed Anne shortly before she died in 2008 told me that Anne had met Barbara, though she didn't say when or how, just that she had found Barbara charming. Was Anne a former colleague? She had taught in Vermont, as Barbara and Nick had briefly. Regardless, Nick appears to have found a steadier wife in Anne. She taught in a Head Start program in Connecticut beginning in 1932, and worked in preschool education throughout her life. Later she volunteered at the Exeter Library. They raised two daughters and had three grandchildren. They would remain married for the rest of Nick's life.

In the days, months, and years following Barbara's disappearance, everyone who swapped theories about what had happened came to this conclusion: that she had run away. It was what they wanted to believe. Marjorie, who was "as close a friend as Bar had, and certainly knew as much as anyone of those last few weeks," told Alice that "Bar boasted to her that she could disappear if she wanted to, and never 'leave a single trace'; that she'd dye her hair, pull out her eyebrows, completely change her personality, and that she could always take care of herself. Marjorie believes she did just that and still lives, really becoming by now a completely different Barbara." Marjorie died in Anaconda, Montana, in 2004 at the age of ninety-three. But her daughter told me that for the rest of her life her mother continued to believe that Barbara had run away of her own free will.

Only Barbara's closest friend, Alice Russell, came to the conclusion that Barbara was dead. The last letters from Barbara in the Columbia archives are written to Alice, and in 1949, ten years after Barbara vanished, Alice wrote to Helen arguing that Barbara couldn't be alive because "it was impossible that she would have treated you, and Sabra, and all whom she loved with cruelty deliberate, for so long a time."

But then one day Alice was sitting on a public bus in Pasadena when she looked up and saw a woman with Barbara's chestnut-colored hair. A jolt of recognition surged through her. She would know that head anywhere. It was Barbara. The woman turned her head slightly to the side and Alice caught a glimpse of her profile. The woman who had so certainly been Barbara transformed into a stranger. All of Alice's hopefulness drained from her. But just like Wilson's experience, this incident made Alice reconsider her previous conviction. It *was* possible. Some part of her expected Barbara to knock on her kitchen door. She told Helen that she had even planned the wire she would send her when Barbara came. She didn't reveal what it would say, probably out of sympathy for Helen, for whom it would have been too much to read: "Bar LIVES!"

Alice began to reevaluate what she thought Barbara was capable of. She wrote that her son-in-law "said she may well have got herself into a situation which she did not want to tell anyone in her former life about. As time went on, it would have grown harder and harder to do so. There *was* a streak of hardness in her—'cruelty,' as Sabra said—that would have acted as an iron deterrent." Barbara could be very stubborn. Maybe she was capable of ditching them all.

"I think she meant to hurt Nick," she theorized. "I think she meant to get away from a situation that was crucifying her, even if it meant cutting herself off from everything and everybody she loved and knew. She had 'jumped hurdles' before," she wrote, quoting a phrase Barbara had used to describe her previous runaway experiences. "With you, I believe we will not now ever see her again; but I think she lives."

Alice was torn by her love for Barbara and her belief that Barbara had committed "an act of egoism." In one letter, she wrote, "I will always love Bar—she was one of the highlights of my life." Rereading Barbara's letters caused Alice acute pain. "Almost every line of hers makes you feel this vivid creature she was. She comes alive again, you *see* her." In other letters to Helen, Alice was harsher, "Bar was a supreme egoist—perhaps it was partly her genius that made her that. She was completely centered in self and blind to the needs of others."

One morning thirteen years after Barbara vanished, Helen woke up and decided to search for Barbara herself. Sitting in her apartment on the Upper West Side, she typed a letter to Nick requesting a detailed account of everything he had done to look for Barbara.

He didn't respond. Helen wrote him a second, more threatening letter, "All this silence on your part almost looks as if you had something to hide concerning Barbara's disappearance." She went on, "You cannot believe I shall sit idle during my last few years and not make whatever effort I can . . ." She appealed to him as a father—his two daughters were young; how would he feel if one of them vanished? She signed off, "Kindness to others is often a rewarding experience to ourselves."

Suddenly Helen didn't trust Nick anymore. She wrote to the Brookline police. "It seems incredible to me that my daughter's husband did not turn the country upside down to find his wife." And then, perhaps sensing that someone could say the same of her, she added, "Certainly, over the years, I have taken it for granted that such a course was being pursued." She explained that she had been busy with an illness and raising Sabra.

Helen wrote to an old sailor friend of Barbara's, who wrote

back to say he hadn't seen her. She met with Barbara's former colleagues. They didn't have anything new to tell her. The police sent Helen a section of a letter from Ruth Isabel Seasbury, who had worked with Barbara at the American Board for Commissioners for Foreign Missions in Brookline. "[Nick] and Barbara are to the best of my knowledge and belief very happily married, but for some time had had a very sharp difference of opinion on a matter which both regarded as of fundamental importance. Barbara had seemed very unhappy about it especially in her last day at home." It's a frustrating letter that raises more questions than it answers. The "matter of fundamental importance" is never revealed—perhaps for propriety's sake, as Seasbury was likely referencing the affair. But what if it was something else? The only new detail the letter reveals is that on the day Barbara vanished, one of the last people to have seen her sensed that she was upset. Barbara would presumably have been agitated at work if she were about to run away from everyone and everything in her life. She might have also been agitated if she was afraid her husband might harm her. Or maybe her unhappiness was a sign that she intended to harm herself. Whatever it was, something was noticeably off.

Without new information, the search soon ended. Alice thought it was useless to try. "Helen, I believe—*let* us believe—that she lives somewhere, still enjoying sunsets and mountains and water." Any time Helen brought up a lead or clue, Alice dismissed it, saying, "But it is no use to think of that—now. The dark waters closed over her long ago." In her letters she seems eager to talk about Barbara, but only up to a point. She does not really want to look for her, or do anything that might reveal new information.

In 1960, Helen contacted a child psychologist, Harold McCurdy, who specialized in child prodigies. She wanted him to analyze Barbara's letters and writings. McCurdy's eleven-year-old daughter had recently died, and he was moved by the story of the brilliant lost girl. Helen and McCurdy decided to cowrite a book about Barbara, which consisted of Barbara's letters alongside McCurdy's analysis, entitled *Barbara: The Unconscious Autobiography of a Child Genius.* If Helen could not have her daughter in the flesh, she would have to settle for her on the page. She was also preserving Barbara's memory for Sabra, who was deeply wounded by her sister's disappearance.

Despite her turbulent childhood, Sabra had done well for herself. She was Phi Beta Kappa at Barnard and became Princeton University's first female graduate student in 1961, entering the history PhD program as a "test case" despite the fact that she already had a master's degree from Columbia and was a history professor at a college in New Brunswick. She married the son of her mother's friend Anne, and they had three children together.

Decades later, Sabra would be haunted by a memory, telling her husband about the time Barbara had come to New York for Thanksgiving, the month before she vanished. Sabra and Helen had walked her to Grand Central Station, where Barbara would take the train back to Boston. They had stood at the crowded station at one end of the platform waving, and Barbara had turned around and waved happily back. Then she had boarded the train. It was the last time they ever saw her. She was gone just like that. It's an unremarkable moment, though perhaps that is the point—how fragile life is, how quickly and unceremoniously someone can be whisked away forever.

At one point or another, Sabra had been left behind by everyone in her family. First her father, then her mother, then Barbara. Alice wrote to Helen, "She did love, she did value Sabra. Sabra must know that." But in the total silence after Barbara disappeared, it must have been hard to remember this. It was easier for Sabra to see herself in the role Barbara had written for her: Eepersip's little sister, a "gigantic burden," the one to whom Eepersip says, "If I were to go back home now, I should just die—even with you."

Years passed and one by one Barbara's friends and family began to die. Wilson died in 1963 and Alice in 1964. In 1970, thirty-one years after Barbara vanished, Sabra and Helen carried several large boxes of Barbara's papers—her letters, novels, poems, education materials, and drawings—to the Rare Book & Manuscript Library at Columbia. The two women sat with the archivist and signed a blue piece of paper giving ownership of Barbara's papers to the university. It was the nearest thing to closure they would ever get. Helen died later that year.

I thought about what Alice had written to Helen: "I have always felt that Nick *could* if he had wanted to, have told us more about his last talk with her and given us perhaps some clue."

There are no letters to or from Nick, no accounts from Nick's perspective. When Barbara described him, she called him "a simple person, and his family is simple." But she had also said he had "unsuspected depths."

Who was Nickerson Rogers and what role did he play in Barbara's disappearance?

TWELVE

When I first saw a photograph of Nick Rogers, I knew instantly it was him. One of Barbara's letters mentioned that his picture had appeared in a 1938 issue of *Life*. I had no guidance beyond that. As I sat in the library and scrolled through the pages on my computer, I came across a photo and stopped. It's not a single image but a triptych, and in each frame Nick is demonstrating Polaroid's technology by holding up two large circular lenses in front of his face. The first frame shows much of his face, but he is squinting in concentration, and his eyes are darkened by shadow. In the second frame, he moves the two lenses closer, like a Venn diagram, and the area where they overlap is semiopaque, obscuring some of his face. In the final frame, he is completely obscured. The photograph seemed to be taunting me.

I decided to make a call I had been dreading. I had tracked down Nick's daughters, and a little over a month earlier I had sent one of them a letter about Barbara. She had either ignored it or never received it. I preferred to believe it was the latter.

I knew very little about Nick's eldest daughter except that she was seventy years old and lived with her husband near a state park in Alaska. It is a striking place, with snowcapped mountains and over twelve hundred square miles of wetlands and boreal forests. I imagined that she shared a love of the outdoors with her father and that this might make her more susceptible to Barbara's story.

My letter, I imagined, might be the first she had ever heard of Barbara. Would her stoic, woodsman father have taken the time to explain his previous life to his daughters? I imagined my letter would ignite a fever of curiosity, that she would pull down boxes from the attic, that maybe she would sit at her computer at night, scouring the Internet for clues about Barbara.

I felt bad about calling up an aging woman in her home with a question I would never state outright, but that would be lurking in the back of my mind: *What was your father capable of?*

I dialed her number quickly and listened to the phone ring. A strong female voice answered.

"Is this Carol?" I asked.

"It is," she said curtly.

"This is Laura Smith. I sent you a letter a month ago about your father's first wife?"

She said nothing.

"Did you get it?" I asked.

"I did."

There was a long pause.

She sighed. "I meant to answer. I meant to write to tell you that my sister and I talked it over for hours and decided nothing good would come from it."

Carol's sister, Melissa,* lived in a French town in the foothills of the Pyrenees. I pictured the two sisters standing in their respective kitchens talking on the phone, looking out on their magnificent vistas. If they had talked for hours, perhaps they had

*Both "Melissa" and "Carol" are pseudonyms.

seriously considered sharing their story. But there was none of that wondering in Carol's voice now. She sounded like a tough lady, the kind who didn't appreciate the prying of strangers and who, when she got an idea in her head, didn't budge.

But then again, she stayed on the phone.

"I feel skeptical of why you're doing this," she said.

"I know," I said. "To be perfectly honest, I don't always feel sure why I'm doing this."

This seemed to soften her slightly. "You know," she said finally, "you're never going to figure out what happened to Bar. Things were different then. Sometimes people just disappear. I know people who have disappeared."

She knew people who had disappeared? I didn't know a single one. My life was filled with people whose whereabouts were known. But more than all her vanished friends, it struck me how she had called Barbara "Bar." It was so familiar, it rolled off her tongue so naturally, like Barbara was just another friend or family member.

"You seem to know a lot about her," I said.

"No, I really don't."

"How did you find out about Barbara?" I asked.

"My mother and father told me," she said.

"When?" I asked.

"When I was a teenager."

"What did your parents say?"

"I don't know. It was a long time ago."

"It must have been strange to hear about this mystery in your father's past. I know that if I had been a teenager, I would have been very interested in a previous life of my father's."

She paused. "I think you're reading too much into it."

Maybe I was.

And then, at some point in our conversation, Carol said two things that stunned me.

She mentioned a private investigator—one who her father had hired—and told me that if that guy couldn't find Barbara, I probably wouldn't be able to either. I told her this was a valid point. But I flagged the detail in my mind. This was the first I had heard of any private investigator. Helen must not have known about it either—or surely she would have contacted him and included her letter to him in the materials she had submitted to the Columbia archive. She was fastidious about Barbara's papers and had included unremarkable letters to police, coworkers, and former friends. One gets the sense, going through Helen's files, that she had deliberately chosen to include all leads, perhaps anticipating that someday someone would seek to retrace her steps. She and Nick were not on good terms and there was no evidence of correspondence between them following her threatening letter in 1952. Perhaps Nick had hired the private investigator after their last correspondence, and she had never known.

Why would you hire a private investigator if you had committed a crime? Perhaps to cover your tracks, to make it look like you were doing everything you could to look for your missing wife. But if that were the case, why hadn't he told her mother he was doing it? I decided I would need to follow up on this, but I would need to tread cautiously, winning Carol's trust slowly over time. She might eventually be more amenable to sharing details, but I could feel her clamming up over the phone and feared that a wrong question would result in a dial tone.

The second surprising thing she told me was that she had sent a box to Barbara's archives at Columbia.

"What was in the box?" I said.

"Letters between my father and Barbara." And then she paused. "They never even acknowledged getting it." She sounded a little hurt. My pulse quickened. Barbara's letters to friends and family had revealed so much. What if I could now see into her relationship with Nick?

Eventually I decided to end the conversation. I knew I might regret it, that I might never hear from Carol again, but I was uncomfortable and wanted to make a gesture of good faith, in the hope that she might be willing to talk to me more later, perhaps when she was feeling less defensive. I had likely ruined her day, dredging up who knows what memories. My interest in Barbara didn't seem to justify another person's pain.

But more than that, I felt a glimmer of excitement. There was a man—a man who had searched for Barbara. And there was a box of letters. And that box, if it still existed, was on Columbia's campus just a short train ride from my apartment. I could picture it, tucked in the corner of some dark and dusty storage room, waiting to be found.

I went back to Columbia and asked a woman at the front desk about the box Nick's daughter had sent. The head archivist, a woman in a neat, conservative dress, came to the reception area and looked at the donation records with me. "Yes," she said, running her finger down the document. "We received a file." The documents were filed with the materials that related to the child psychologist's book, under the label "Nickerson Rogers Papers," which I instantly recognized. I had seen those papers before and it had never occurred to me that these could possibly be the papers Carol had described. I asked to see the file again, in case I was mistaken. When she brought a thin folder to my table, I was disappointed. These weren't personal letters. They were essays Nick had written in a college classics course, years before he met Barbara. They didn't have anything to do with Barbara. They didn't really have anything to do with him.

I called Carol back. There was no answer so I left a message. I told her that Columbia had the papers, but they weren't as she had described. I asked her to call me back. I didn't hear anything, and after a few weeks I called again, saying I wanted to talk only about the papers and the private investigator and nothing else. I heard nothing. I sent a long letter explaining that I wanted to know more about the investigator. Still nothing. I never heard from her again.

THIRTEEN

Our first summer in Brooklyn P.J. went away for a weekend to visit a friend in Chicago. When he returned we went to a café in the West Village for dinner and sat at the bar. P.J. seemed electric, bursting with something to tell me.

"What's going on?" I said.

He explained that early on in the trip, his friend* had revealed to him that he had been curious about having sexual experiences with people in addition to his longtime partner. It wasn't about dating other people; in fact, he wanted her to be part of the experiences. He said he wanted to explore all aspects of sexuality with her, to share everything with her.

I was shocked. This was one of the last couples I would have expected this from. They seemed so paired, always cooking together, preferring a night at home reading to a rowdy night out. They were traditional seeming, cautious by nature. But then I stiffened, thinking, *Oh God, I hope P.J. doesn't want to do that.*

"Is this what you want?" I whispered, looking around to make sure no one could hear us. The restaurant was loud and crowded, but suddenly I felt exposed and certain that the balding man in the black glasses next to us was listening.

*Minor details of this friend's story have been changed to protect his privacy.

"Well, on some level," P.J. said. "But jealousy seems inevitable. In any case, talking about it honestly seems like a good thing."

I didn't like the glimmer in his eye. I signaled to the waiter that we were going to need more wine.

"I don't think I could ever do it," I said. Though our friends' situation had nothing to do with us, it felt personal. Anything I said about their potential nonmonogamy seemed a comment on our own relationship.

An open relationship struck me as messy and dangerous. What was the point? Why imperil a marriage if things were going well? I looked around the restaurant and suddenly felt overwhelmed. The waiters burst through the kitchen doors, weaving between the crowded tables with trays stacked with food. There were plates and wineglasses everywhere and everything was in motion—people putting on and taking off jackets, swinging open the front door, eating, laughing, and gesticulating. I hoped we would keep the conversation just that, a thrill to inject into our imaginations, but not something we would actually do. I could tell P.J. was enjoying talking about it, and I had to admit that my heart was beating a little faster, though I couldn't tell if it was from exhilaration or panic.

Eventually the fuzzy warmth of the wine relaxed me. Maybe it was fun to spend the evening in a lively restaurant locked in salacious conversation. The idea of P.J. feeling desires and keeping them secret from me gave them an unsavory, illicit quality, and cast me in the role of naive spouse and thought police. I didn't want to be someone he had to hide things from. The touchiness of the topic seemed a reason to probe further, otherwise we'd be hiding things from each other and, perhaps even more insidiously, from ourselves. In fact, our friends' openness seemed to be a sign of their intense closeness. How could they not talk openly about these desires? How could we not? Of course I had felt fleeting attractions in the past, but anything more than harmless flirtation was unthinkable. I could honestly say I had never truly been tempted, always dismissing the idea before it could blossom. Our attractions to others had been admitted only guiltily in the past. I felt suddenly pardoned from guilt.

A few weeks later when I asked P.J. what was going on with our friends, he had nothing new to report. They seemed in no rush to make decisions about monogamy, and I took comfort in their lack of urgency. There's no reason to do anything drastic, I thought. It's fun to talk about but maybe better not to do, I told myself.

P.J. and I spent the winter holed up in our tiny apartment, rushing on errands with our hoods up and heads down to avoid the biting wind. I applied for two journalism fellowships, one in Germany and Poland for the first part of the summer and one in the Canadian Rockies for the second part. I thought I would be lucky to get one, but a few months later, I found out I got both. P.J. and I would be spending the entire summer apart. On the rare occasions when he had to travel for work, I always woke up in the middle of the night confused. Where was he? I couldn't picture getting on an airplane and sitting next to a stranger, shopping in the grocery store for one. I was equal parts nervous and thrilled.

In the spring, the air warmed and being outside was possible again. There were tulips in the nearby park and little green buds on the tree outside our window. People filled the sidewalks and restaurants opened their windows. The days became longer and people stayed out later, savoring the balmy weather.

I didn't think much about our conversation until we went out to dinner with another friend and his new girlfriend. Sitting at a small table at the back of the dark restaurant, they told us they were in an open relationship. I tried not to look shocked, wanting to be more open minded than that. Their relationship was the only topic of discussion. Our friend's girlfriend, whom I'll call Julia, is tall and beautiful with an aura of calm that masks her blunt talk and pointed questions. As she talked, I admired her total lack of conversational prudishness. Our friend, whom I'll call Ryan, seemed to be glowing in her presence. As one beer turned into four and P.J. and I continued to pepper them with questions, I had the impression that they were being very patient with us, rehashing well-trodden ground that they didn't need to bother discussing with their more progressive friends.

"But what if you fall in love?" I asked Julia. "What if he decides to leave you for someone else?"

"If he finds someone else he thinks he would be better with, maybe he should be with that person," she said.

I couldn't argue with that logic, though I wasn't sure I could muster the same magnanimity. I wanted P.J. to be with me no matter what—even if he would thrive more with someone else. Was there not something to be said for agreeing to stick with one relationship and trying to make that work? How could you really invest yourself in something if it seemed expendable? Julia and Ryan argued that they didn't see their relationship as expendable, but they didn't want to be constrained by the suppression of their real feelings. I found their ease in talking about a potential separation to be deeply unnerving. *He's sitting right there,* I felt like reminding her.

While I admired their comfort with uncertainty, I was

skeptical that their arrangement could possibly work for very long. I pictured them casually reviewing their calendars at breakfast. "Next Tuesday, I'll be with Frank, so how about Wednesday for dinner?" I imagined her saying. "And on your way home from Jennifer, could you grab a couple of things at the store?" It made my stomach churn.

When I tried to isolate what I found so frightening about their arrangement, I settled on an imagined scene: I was alone in a quiet room at night, knowing P.J. was with someone else, waiting for him to come home. Perhaps I was trying to read or watch television to pass the time, but mostly I was just feeling abandoned.

I turned to Ryan, "So how does this work? She says, I have a date tonight, and she just goes off, and you're sitting at home?"

"Well, I might have a date too," he said.

"But how do you *feel*?" I asked, narrowing my eyes at him.

"Usually jealous, but that can be hot."

I told myself I had always tried to avoid jealousy and couldn't imagine doing something to encourage that feeling. But then I realized this wasn't entirely true. When another person found P.J. attractive, I felt proud. Someone could see what I saw in him. But there was something else too. Jealousy was a confusing tangle of emotions. Was one of the threads of that tangle arousal? There were times when I could recall relishing jealousy, when I had enjoyed looking across a room and seeing P.J. talking to some beautiful girl. It was a strangely satisfying burn.

My questions were endless. Did they tell each other everything? How did they make plans? What if one person got upset? How did the other person react? Were there rules and if so, what were they? But with each answer I was less satisfied than before.

It seemed like some crucial piece of information that allowed me to envision their lives was missing. Maybe I'm just a monogamist, I thought. We finished our drinks and said goodnight. As I watched them walk down the darkened street, I was left standing on the curb feeling very old fashioned. And something was nagging at me.

A few weeks later, an entirely different friend suggested to his girlfriend that they have an open relationship. She said no. He broke up with her. Their situation seemed different. They weren't well matched for a host of reasons that were obvious to everyone except them. When the boyfriend proposed the open relationship, he wasn't ready to break up, but he wanted to start the leaving process. The suggestion was the antechamber to splitting up. Their situation revealed something that I had always believed about relationships—that if you truly loved someone, if your relationship was strong and you were with "the right person," then you wouldn't want anyone else. Your desires would be magically replaced by eternal satisfaction. Now this struck me as a fairy tale.

Suddenly, I wanted to talk about the possibility of sex with others all the time and I was the one initiating the conversation. I felt our discussions unexpectedly drawing us closer, as though now I truly had access to P.J.'s deepest fears and desires. All of the erotic talk flared our imaginations and desire for one another. We were coconspirators, endlessly plotting together. Imagining giving him his freedom was liberating for me. We had never been very jealous or controlling, but now I could see all the subtle ways

I had occasionally played the role of jailer or punisher or parent, and I was relieved not to feel that way. I enjoyed my imagined freedom too. It gave me a brisk joyful feeling, like a kid on summer break.

We talked about the people we were attracted to, about the scenarios we could imagine, and potential rules *if* we were to do it. I was afraid P.J. would fall in love with someone else. He had a very visceral reaction to the idea of my having sex with someone else. My body was my own, he told himself. But he couldn't shake the feeling that my body was also his. I enjoyed this possessiveness and the feelings of belonging it inspired, but I also wondered: was he not, on some level, trying to tuck me away from the world? I found the idea of his having sex with another woman surprisingly untroubling. It's just bodies, I thought. The power we had previously attributed to sex suddenly seemed overblown and puritanical. I was much more worried about the fact that we were creating the exact circumstances in which he might fall in love with someone else. He's thinking about sex and I'm thinking about love, I realized. How predictable.

I considered that our marriage was perhaps the only frontier I had been unwilling to explore. What was I afraid of finding? Three years before, in an airplane somewhere over the Pacific Ocean, I had told myself that my relationship with P.J. was the only thing I would not risk, but now I realized that I had said that out of fear, that I needed one thing—one person—to pin me down to the world. I had always envisioned adventure as traveling somewhere, but now I wondered if an interpersonal adventure could be as, if not more, exciting.

Simone de Beauvoir argued that her greatest accomplishment of all—never mind that staple of Second Wave feminism, *The*

Second Sex—was her relationship with Jean-Paul Sartre, which had famously bucked monogamy. Vanessa Bell, Virginia Woolf's sister, had lived in an old East Sussex farmhouse with her husband, Clive Bell, with whom she had two children; a former paramour, Roger Fry; and Duncan Grant, the dashing artist she was desperately in love with but who was rather inconveniently gay. Duncan's lover, David Garnett, who would later marry Vanessa's daughter with Duncan, could often be found at the farmhouse too. It was, at first glance, a household pregnant with disaster, love triangles heaped upon love triangles. But in this often painful, sometimes downright disorienting domestic tangle, Vanessa had reimagined what it meant to be family. No one could say that her life was not brimming with love, that she was not living intensely. Amelia Earhart had written to her fiancé, George Putnam, "I shall not hold you to any midaeval code of faithfulness to me, nor shall I consider myself bound to you similarly. . . . Please let us not interfere with each others' work or play." They would be bound, but not bound. It reminded me of Barbara's "the first requisite of a happy marriage is not to be married." Were there ways to be bound, but free?

I admired these women's willingness to tinker and experiment, to find lives and relationships that better suited them. In an institution where the prevailing measure of success is longevity, merely surviving, slogging through together across the grueling decades to arrive at a finish line which is in theory marked by death, these women were searching for other metrics. They brought the relentless probing and creative vigor that they applied to their work to their lives. Their bravery befitted the brevity of life. I wanted to be that radical, that pioneering, that willing to view my life as a work in progress, not a fait accompli. Having an open marriage suddenly seemed a more authentic arrangement. It acknowledged attraction rather than trying to stuff it away in the back drawer of your consciousness. We knew there would be pain. But avoiding pain at all cost seemed like a dull way to live.

I found myself thinking about Barbara on the Appalachian Trail. How much of her adventure was about the trail and how much of it was about Nick? The more intoxicating adventure was probably that of falling in love, of letting yourself be vulnerable to someone new. Nick was the true undiscovered country. It was his "unsuspected depths" that had drawn her. To her mind, it wasn't a real adventure if you knew exactly where you would turn up. A real adventure was a little dangerous. It might upend your life.

To Barbara, life afforded few opportunities for "high adventure," as she called it. "I've had one or two fairly high adventures, and am convinced that they are worth all kinds of sweat and pain and other troubles; in fact, they are the only things really worth suffering for." When the moment arose, you had to seize it. "If you fully realize what a messy world it is," she had written to Alice, "and are reconciled to certain facts, such as continual change and permanence in nothing, why then you can have a surprisingly good time."

A friend once joked that we all have a little Victorian lady living inside of us who wags her finger at any suggestion of deviance, especially of the sexual variety. I was enjoying shocking the little Victorian lady who lived inside of me. In fact, I wanted to cast her out.

I was twenty-nine and married, well on my way to having 2.4 children before my ovaries wore out, and it was all a little too home-catalogue-inspired for my taste. As P.J. and I talked about the possibility of opening our marriage, I thought, *yes,* I want to be the type of person who is not too chickenshit to try this.

"If there's a problem, we'll just talk about it," we assured one another. I worried that there might be something you could not talk your way out of—say, for example, feelings—but I told myself that willpower could, if necessary, prevail. It was P.J. I was worried about. What if he lost control?

We developed a new language to discuss the possibility of sex with other people. It was not, *should we fuck other people?* It was, *should we be open?* "Being open" had a nice sound to it, as if we would just open a jar and lovely things would come fluttering out. Other times it was "the arrangement," like a friendly business deal struck up over lunch. Our endless hours discussing and wondering in coffee shops, at dinner tables, or walking down the sidewalks of our neighborhood were an attempt to intellectualize the rawest parts of ourselves and study them with scientific zeal, and in so doing assure ourselves that we were in control. I hoped that dressing our desires in finer clothing—the clothing of intellectual inquiry—might elevate them to something worthy of pursuit.

Historical examples hardly suggested it was a path to un-alloyed bliss, though. Many people have wondered about the happiness of Simone de Beauvoir. Sartre was a far more prolific philanderer. Did this create a power imbalance? Was parity ever possible? Amelia Earhart didn't live long enough to find out if her arrangement could work. Vanessa Bell's daughter with Duncan, Angelica, wrote a pained and critical memoir about growing up in such an unconventional household. And what of Vanessa Bell's husband, Clive? Was his life so brimming with love? Had she, in filling her cup, drained his?

I left for Germany and Poland with these issues unresolved. On return, as my departure for Canada loomed, the question became more pressing. I was, after all, going to Banff to write about Barbara's marriage; it seemed an ideal time to think deeply about our own. P.J. and I would be spending several weeks apart, a less problematic time to experiment. And we both had the sense that if we didn't do it then, we probably never would. We felt closer than ever. All the excitement we had built up over the last few weeks would drain suddenly from our lives, and that idea was extremely unappealing.

It would be an understatement to say that P.J. struggles with decisions. He is constitutionally indecisive, feeling compelled to talk about the pros and cons of every decision ad nauseam. I am constitutionally decisive, often impulsive, preferring swift action to endless consideration. One afternoon, we were on the telephone while he was traveling for a few days for work. "Let's do it," I said, feeling a flush of excitement. I wanted to be the one who said it first, not the one who agreed or lagged behind. "I give you my blessing," I said in my best approximation of a papal dispensation.

I was joking but also not. I knew he would need an official pardon because he was raised Catholic and though his Catholic days were long past, a scrupulousness remained. There would be times when he would need, for the sake of his conscience, to recall that I had given him permission. The legalese of that conversation allowed me not to think too directly about what I was saying. I was giving my husband permission to sleep with other people. I was giving myself permission.

"Okay, great!" P.J. joked, having not yet given me his blessing. Of course the joke contained a kernel of truth—that really he didn't want me to sleep with other people, that he wished there were some way he could sleep with other people and I would not. I knew it because I felt the same way. But we were striving not just for freedom but also for fairness. Still I hoped that whatever he did, he would always choose me in the end.

There was another long pause.

"I give you my blessing," he said.

I looked at men differently after that. Sitting in a coffeehouse, I saw a man reading a book. I wondered about him. How did he take his coffee? Did he have a sister?

On a train after a night of drinking with friends, I saw a dark-haired man a few seats farther down the car. He was alone and lost in thought. What did he look like when he was sleeping? How would he touch me? Did he prefer sex gentle or rough?

I knew that I was lucky to have found love at all, that I was lucky to have P.J., and it was perhaps ungrateful and greedy to want more. And yet to dismiss my blossoming desire seemed a tragic amputation. I felt as though I had stumbled upon a whole new wing of my house. My world suddenly expanded.

One night shortly before leaving, I put on a long black dress that I knew P.J. liked, and we went out to dinner at a cozy Italian restaurant near our apartment. We sat close together at the bar, drinking white wine. We kept grabbing each other's hands. P.J. looked at me. Was he trying to imagine what it might be like to see me for the first time—to be a stranger? The danger of a dalliance had piqued our awareness of each other. Did he look a little sad? His face shifted suddenly, now looking excited.

As I leaned across to him in the low-lit bar, I had the sense that we were partners in crime. P.J. whispered in my ear, "I want you all for myself," and then he laughed a strange, truncated laugh. "Oh, man, what am I doing?" he groaned and laughed again. In his tone, I heard desperation. He didn't really have me anymore, and he knew it. He gripped my hand.

"We don't have to do this, you know," I heard myself say.

"Yeah, cancel the whole thing," he said. He kissed my hand again.

I told myself we couldn't turn back. If we called it off, we would always wonder, and the wondering would torment us. We looked at each other, blinking almost wistfully, shaking our heads and occasionally laughing because it was all so absurd.

Two weeks later, I boarded a plane to Canada.

FOURTEEN

I was told that in Banff people lose their minds. It may have something to do with the altitude—Banff is a small ski town in western Canada that sits at around 4,500 feet above sea level. Or perhaps it's the dizzying views of sharp, rock-faced mountains protruding above the tree line reminding people of their mortality and inspiring them to do things they normally wouldn't. I had been warned that people couldn't sleep there and was told to arm myself with eye masks, earplugs, melatonin, or something stronger. Marriages end here, a man told me. I thought I detected a note of satisfaction in his voice. A woman told me that when First Nations people had come to the hill overlooking what would become the town of Banff, it had given them an ominous feeling and they had moved on. "Bad mojo," she said. People seemed to love Banff perhaps precisely because of the chaos it brought into their lives.

At the Calgary airport tall men in Stetson hats, chaps, and tight-fitting jeans were performing a country song in the lobby and cowboy memorabilia was everywhere: lassos, boots, large hats. My arrival coincided with Stampede, a ten-day rodeo with events such as calf roping and ladies' barrel racing. I heaved my large bag off the belt. A lone traveler. The thought gave me a prickle of satisfaction. P.J. would pick me up from Banff to go camping for two weeks at the end of the summer, but until then, we would essentially be leading separate lives.

I took the shuttle into Banff with Taylor, a writer friend from New York, who would also be attending the residency. As he and I talked, the flat plains of Calgary gradually rose up into the Canadian Rockies. Surrounding the town were dense alpine woods with hiking trails that ran along steep rock faces, glacial rivers, and thin spires that protruded skyward like misshapen fingers, known as hoodoos. The shuttle pulled into the arts center. The sounds of stringed instruments being tuned and opera singers rehearsing filled the air. A greeter showed us to the welcome center and told us that elk and mule deer with fuzzy antlers occasionally wandered through people's front yards and that we should stay away from them during mating season. Solitary trail jogging was discouraged on account of the grizzlies, cougars, and wolves. We were assigned to studio cabins nestled in the woods, where we would work, and hotel rooms, where we would sleep. I took a deep breath of the mountain air and thought of New York with its car fumes and grimy sidewalks. Suddenly I couldn't remember why I lived there.

At dinner that evening, Taylor and I met the other six residents. I immediately liked our cohort: a couple of academics, a crime reporter, a strange wiry young poet turned nonfiction writer, and a magazine writer with feline eyes and a deadpan expression, but I liked Michael best of all. He was handsome, broad shouldered, and charming. He dressed like an Italian from the 1950s, which gave him the well-kempt but carefree look of a gentleman perpetually on vacation. We talked about psychopaths, which we had both spent time researching for stories. I took note of him and tucked the thought away.

Roy Wilson Follett reading to Barbara, circa 1916.

Barbara Follett as a child.

Barbara in the woods around the time she wrote her first novel, *The House Without Windows.*

An undated photo of Barbara at her typewriter. Wilson said he taught her to type when she was three years old; Helen that she taught her when she was five.

Barbara and her sister Sabra on Lake Sunapee, circa 1924. The Folletts spent many happy summers in a rented cabin on the lake. The place was particularly significant to Barbara, who loved canoeing, hiking, and swimming with her father there.

leave the deer just yet, and was determined not to put on her shoes and stockings again. So she decided to stay in the soft grass until her feet were toughened; and then she tought she could go up that wonderful peak over which the sun rose in clouds of glory. Before Eepersip had danced long she walked down toward the great precipice again, with her shoes and stockings under her arms. The instant she got there a madness came upon her, and whizz! two shoes and two stockings were flying through the air at a tremendous rate, and landed far below, while Eepersip, glad to get rid of them, coolly walked back thinking that her feet were already tougher than before because of that bold act. When she got back she decided to rest awhile, then walk in the opposite direction and see what was at the northern end of the glade. So when she got rested she started off that way, with the doe and her fawn trotting by her side. At last she came to the slope of the mountain on that side. But this slope, instead of being a steep precipice, was a gradually sloping grassy bank, down which she went. The doe and the fawn followed some distance; then they turned back, letting Eepersip go on alone. But when she got to the bottom she began to see houses; and so, deciding that that wasn't the side for her, she ran back as fast as she could.

Meanwhile Mr. and Mrs. Eigleen were wondering in vain where their poor child had gone. At first they hadn't thought much about her, for she had been lost in the woods several times before and had always found her way home safely. But when it came to be gone two or three whole days, why, they were not sure that they were awake! The child must be starving, and who knew what a tender morsel to some prowling animal she might be by this time? So they began to grieve greatly over their loss, for they loved Eepersip dearly.

Before they had missed Eepersip very long, a poor woman and her husband had climbed that part of Mount Varcrobis. Nobody in the village down below cared much for Mr. and Mrs. Ikisfield, as they were called; and they had decided to elsewhere, and seeing the cottage and they friends. The Eigleens took pity on them, and at last persuaded them to live in the little cottage in the woods, and to let the Eigleens themselves go to the house of friends of theirs, the Wraspanes. It was the Wraspanes rhododendron

Barbara in the White Mountains in 1926.

Barbara aboard the *Vigilant* in 1929. It was on this journey that she met Ed Anderson, the shipmate with whom she carried on a romantic correspondence for many years.

Barbara and Helen during their South Seas voyage (1929 or 1930) after Wilson abandoned the family. The trip was tumultuous, with mother and daughter fighting often. Helen recalled their adventure fondly in her books *Stars to Steer By* and *Magic Portholes,* which Barbara edited. Their letters present a darker story.

Helen Thomas Follett,
circa 1935.

Alice Russell and
Barbara in Pasadena,
California, circa 1930.
Though there were
decades between
them, Alice, a thriller
writer, was one of
Barbara's closest
friends and
correspondents.

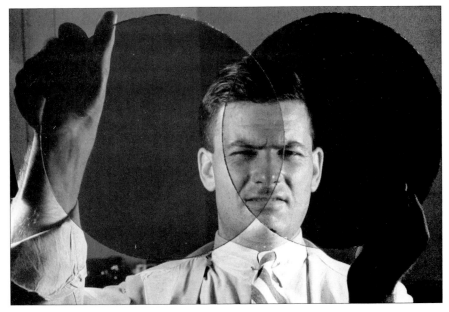

In the year before she vanished, Barbara and her husband Nickerson Rogers were often apart. Nick, shown here in a 1938 issue of *Life* magazine, worked as a technician at Polaroid, which required him to travel all over the country. That same year, she vacationed without him—a fact he would later cite when filing for divorce.

Barbara camping with Nick Rogers in Maine during the summer of 1932. Barbara left her job in New York at the height of the Depression to spend four months hiking in the newly formed Appalachian Trail.

The last known photograph of Barbara, date unknown.

I soon settled in to a routine, writing in the mornings and jogging with Taylor on the Hoodoo Trail or into town in the afternoons. Taylor talked constantly. As we ran along the icy Bow River, we talked about my marriage and Taylor's relationships. I heard in minute detail the life stories of every one of his girl-friends, all of whom seemed to be named Sarah or Kate. Some-times we would work through our story ideas—though mostly it was Taylor's story ideas, which meant we spent a lot of time talking about mania because that was what he was most interested in. I learned about the discovery of lithium, the salt that Taylor said had saved his life, and about Emil Kraepelin, the German psychologist who first defined manic depression. Sometimes talk-ing so much about mania made me feel a little manic, but I couldn't tell if it was runner's high or the effect Taylor was having on me. He and I established an agreement that if his talking got to be too much, I would tell him to "turn off the Taylor tap," which I did a few times.

After our run I usually called P.J., then I'd work again until dinner, after which my new friends and I drank heavily and oc-casionally went to an opera or an art show, or went back to one of our studios to dance and talk.

My life in New York soon began to fade. I tried to imagine our block in Brooklyn, the coffee shop on the corner, the Yemeni sandwich place, and the chatter of sidewalk conversation. It began to seem remote and alien. Friends called and I didn't pick up. When one sent an e-mail saying, "Let's find a time to catch up," I felt irritated. Their calls and texts were an intrusion on our perfect self-contained world in Banff. I didn't want to be re-minded of a world outside of trail runs, my studio, or the nights spent drinking and talking in our studio decks in the woods, because each call and e-mail reminded me that this was not going to last, that soon I would have to return to my small apartment, to grocery lists, and to the sink that seemed always to be filled with dishes.

Though I avoided other phone calls, P.J. and I still talked on the phone every day, often twice a day. It didn't feel like an encroachment because he understood when I had to jump off suddenly because someone had knocked on the studio door. He was enjoying his freedom as well. At night, I would call him while I was getting dressed.

"Where are you going tonight?" I'd ask.

"A bar," he'd say. He hadn't been with anyone yet, and the possibility charged our conversations with tantalizing danger. I wasn't really his anymore. He wasn't really mine. I felt an urge to cling to him, to retreat back into our marital den like a cautious mammal, but I stopped myself and felt a rush. *It's just bodies,* I thought, feeling scorn for past selves that would have been horrified by this attitude. My life, which had always been bogged down by fears of disappointing other people, now suddenly seemed unencumbered.

Something subtle had changed in the way I interacted with the people around me. I felt more at ease in the presence of strangers, not like a beetle scurrying off to avoid their notice. Now if a man was looking at me, I could look back. Why had I given them the power of evaluation when I had just as much of a right to evaluate them?

Previously, I had found walking in public a solitary experience. I was almost startled one day in the grocery when a woman asked me if the polenta I was buying was any good. I looked around the aisle, assuming she must be speaking to someone else.

She had pierced some tacit agreement that when you're in public, you will mind your own business.

Now I wanted to interact with people—all people. It seemed not just that my marriage had opened up but that my world had. Single friends had remarked on the impenetrability of couples before. I told myself that while I had noticed pairs lurking near the hors d'oeuvres table disengaged from the party around them, P.J. and I weren't like that. But of course we were. Couples exist in their own little self-sufficient world, and people sense this and retreat.

I asked Taylor what he thought about this. "Look," he said, "when you're hanging out with a couple, the conversation you're going to have is different than if you talked to them one-on-one." I conceded that this was true. I felt that people treated me differently when P.J. was around. And there were many times over the past few years when, faced with a Saturday night, I would think to myself, "What's the point? I'd rather just talk to P.J." There was something beautiful about that. But it was also stifling.

I considered the idea that nuclear families suffered from a similar isolation—in the creation of a unit, of one house separate from other houses, was the implicit exclusion of all others. This was what bothered me most about wandering around my neighborhood as a kid. Inside the houses, the kids and parents seemed lonely, cut off from the rest of the world. I didn't want the intimacy of a small group to remove me from everyone else.

One night, a few of us went to a dance performance. Michael and I got separated (perhaps intentionally) from the rest of the group and sat near the back of the darkly lit performance hall.

He was wearing a checkered blazer and I remember being aware of his body in the seat next to mine. His knee grazed mine. I could smell the faint scent of white wine and his cologne. I could sense him looking at me and heard him breathing in the dark.

The dance performance was choreographed by a man whose young daughter had died in a house fire, and the dance was loosely based on that night. Watching the dancers writhe on stage, fling their bodies about, and call out, I was moved. My chest swelled as the protagonist clawed at the walls. The music and my own pulse pounded in my ears. I decided I had never seen a better performance of anything. I decided I would sleep with Michael.

At the end of the performance we joined the bustle of the crowd, our shoulders brushing. We ran into someone we knew, greeted her, and quickly moved on. Michael seemed to want to avoid other people as much as I did. Their presence was an intrusion on our intimacy.

"Michael," I said coolly as the crowd thinned out.

"Yes?"

"P.J. and I have an arrangement." He looked at me and I sensed that he knew exactly what I meant. That night, my life was my creation.

The next day I sat in the studio trying to write. I had called P.J. on the phone after leaving Michael's room and told him what had happened. I was troubled that I couldn't really read his reaction as we'd had only a few minutes to talk. Was his voice cold because he was within earshot of friends? Or was it something else? I hoped that P.J. would sleep with someone quickly. I sensed that if he didn't I would begin to feel guilty.

I heard a knock on the studio door. It was Michael, bringing a Danish and coffee. He was both gentle and cautious, trying not to overwhelm me, but pleased by what had happened. At dinner with a group of friends, I felt his foot brush mine, and I brushed his back.

Later that night, we danced to Paul Simon's *Graceland* on the porch of one of our studios. Michael was a good dancer, whisking whomever he was dancing with confidently around the porch, laughing. I liked the way he smoked a cigarette, how he brought his whole open hand to his mouth, tilted his head thoughtfully downward, and breathed in. My ex-boyfriend had been a smoker and I had hated it, but now, inexplicably, I liked watching Michael smoke.

"You're a shitty dancer, but I don't care," Michael said, pulling me to him when no one was looking.

By the third day, he told me he was in love, and by the sixth I believed him. Late one afternoon, we walked to downtown Banff. We sat on slate stairs that led to the bank of the Bow River. In the distance, we could see a field and a large stony mountain rising above the tree line. The sun was setting.

"This place is ugly as shit," Michael said, and I laughed.

"I have to tell you something," he said, suddenly looking solemn.

"Okay, tell me," I said, feeling alarmed.

"I want you to know that we could have a life together, that to me, this isn't just some fling. I don't have a ring, but I'll marry you."

I reminded him that I was already married, and that we had known each other for only a couple of weeks.

"But when you know, you know," he said. I wasn't sure what to say, suddenly feeling a bit overwhelmed by his emotions. "Just say that you understand that I'm serious," he said.

"I understand," I said.

I remember thinking that his feelings were getting out of control and that it was a good thing my own sense of control was still so firmly in place. But a few nights later, we spoke about our families, and he told me about the first time he remembered seeing his sister. He was three years older than she was, and she was sleeping in her room. He opened the door and tiptoed over to her crib. Peeking over the edge, he was struck by a pang of awe. "There was this wonderful, magical creature right there in my house. We've been best friends ever since," he said. I was moved in a way that felt tectonic. I turned and looked at him, considering him in a way I hadn't before. I wanted to be near someone who thought and felt things like that.

In the afternoons we worked together in my studio. We would share drafts or discuss our work. He was writing about a poet who was imprisoned in Saudi Arabia. If a line wasn't reading right, he would give it to me and I'd suggest a change. He would read a paragraph and I would tell him how it sounded.

"I want to do this forever," Michael said, "us working side by side." I bristled. I already had a person I shared my work with.

This was not how things were supposed to go. I had imagined friends with benefits, but without realizing it in a matter of days I had somehow slipped into a serious relationship. My calls to P.J. became less frequent, which I told myself was because of our conflicting schedules. He had become somewhat nocturnal, staying out at bars or concerts with friends and sleeping late. Though his work was lighter in the summer, there was still some, and he had to cram it into his busy socializing schedule. He hadn't slept with anyone yet.

One night, all the journalists and a few of the opera singers went to a karaoke bar downtown that had a mechanical bull. We drank a lot, rode the bull, and some of the opera singers sang rock ballads. An alumnus from a previous year was there, a journalist from a subarctic town in Canada. He was handsome with delicate, fair features. He pulled me onto the dance floor.

"I'm camping by the lake," he whispered in my ear. "Come swimming with me."

I laughed. "Oh, I can't," I said. "I'm married and I'm sleeping with Michael." It was only when I said those words that the strangeness of my situation struck me. Swimming with strangers at night was the kind of thing I had envisioned when P.J. and I had talked about nonmonogamy. It was supposed to be harmless and light. Our lovers would return to their subarctic towns, and we would never hear from them again. But I hadn't even considered going with the subarctic journalist, not because of P.J., but because of Michael. I had noticed him sulking near the bar, and now he was nowhere in sight. Not only did I not want to go swimming at the campsite, I felt I couldn't. I was a monogamous adulteress. All of my inclinations were driving toward more intimacy, not less.

"That's insane!" the journalist said with a laugh. He shook his head and slipped out of the bar.

Michael came back, looking stormy and smelling of cigarettes. I told him what had happened and his face became grave. "Are you going with him?" he asked.

"No," I said. "I'm going with you."

Michael and I began to refer to our relationship as our Banff marriage. He was now living almost exclusively in my hotel room and often worked in my studio. We learned each other's sleeping habits. Sleep has always been fragile for me, but now in Banff, it was especially brittle. If he sensed me tossing and turning, he'd jump out of bed to grab a melatonin or my eye mask. If he snored, I rolled him over on his side. We developed our own language, our own nicknames. I noticed something in his ear and stuck my finger in and pulled it out, a gesture that, while kind of gross, struck him as romantic. It suggested comfort, a lowering of barriers between bodies. He liked watching me get ready because it was something that no one else saw, a vulnerable moment before my presentation to the outside world was complete.

"You're mine," he would say.

His possessiveness both aroused and repelled me. I thought, no, I am no one's.

I saw my relationship with Michael as a beautiful little terrarium: a self-sufficient ecosystem that had no bearing on the outside world. There were none of the questions about the future that often weigh down the beginnings of relationships. I wasn't constantly reading his behaviors for red flags. I didn't wonder if he would have ear hair when he got older. I didn't read his flair for the dramatic as a sign that we were emotionally incompatible. When I brought him on a run and he cursed, panted, and sweated the whole way, complaining that he just wanted a cigarette and a beer, I found it charming. I stopped running and started walking with him instead and didn't worry about whether this meant we were ill matched. I wasn't playing soothsayer, trying to divine the desires of my future self and how it would match up with his future self. We slipped away from our studios to hike the hoo-doos. One night we told friends we were working late and went to a Cajun restaurant in town. I imagined strangers seeing us and thinking we were married and felt a pulse of pleasure. Then I imagined their horrified faces when we said no, we were having an affair, and felt an equally appealing pulse of pleasure.

We walked through the residential areas of Banff holding hands, pointing out which little cottages we liked best. "Are we house hunting?" I asked. "Yes," he said. It was only in the ter-rarium that I could indulge a house fantasy. In the terrarium, my house was beautiful. It was a white clapboard cottage with peri-winkle hydrangea and a pair of rain boots by the front door. I could search for a house with Michael and imagine living there, precisely because I knew it would never happen. But then another voice in my head chimed in, *what if it could?*

I had begun to dread my phone calls with P.J. The church outside our apartment was under construction, and he said the early-morning drilling was driving him insane. His moods were impos-sible to predict. Sometimes he was loving and reassuring. Other times I heard a robotic stoicism in his voice. His questions were explicit and made me uncomfortable. Even though total transpar-ency had been our agreement, I found it tempting to avoid men-tioning things I thought might hurt him. At the same time, I wanted to know all the nuances of his experiences with other people. A few girls had given him their numbers. Each time, I wanted to know, What was she like? Had she approached him or had he approached her? What was it like—*really*? I craved a complete record of their interactions, and P.J.'s answers to my questions were never satisfying. Some crucial element always seemed murky. Were we subtly but deliberately obscuring our experiences from each other? And if so, was that wrong?

At other times P.J. sounded enlivened by our conversations. There was warmth between us and we seemed to be bringing others into our intimacy. "There is no doubt," he said at one point, "that there is more love in our lives now." He had grown closer to a group of our friends and was enjoying the expansive sense of belonging this gave him.

I never knew which mood I would find him in, and often I would find him in both moods on the same day, even in the same moment. Our conversations were riddled with contradictions. "I have to let go of you to have you," P.J. said. We settled into a routine of one bad and one good conversation every day. Occasionally, during the bad conversations, we would discuss the possibility of calling off the experiment. But I had the sense that a chain of events beyond our control was in motion. Like skydivers in free fall, we could not get back on the plane. Besides, how could we stop when P.J. hadn't slept with anyone yet? Of course *I* could have stopped and given him a pass to sleep with someone, but I didn't want to stop. I was jittery on the phone, anxious that he would say something that would make it necessary for me to end things with Michael. The summer would be over soon enough and I was greedy for the time we had left.

Michael would occasionally stun me by crying. I would be talking and look over only to find silent tears running down his face. I had always found displays of emotion disconcerting and slightly awkward, but watching him cry I was touched by his contradictions, the way he was both gentle and strong. I didn't want to admit how quickly my feelings for him had changed, how precipitously I had fallen in love. Now when Michael told me he loved me, I said it back.

Taylor, meanwhile, was producing thousands of words a day, writing until the early morning hours. He had stopped sleeping entirely. His eyes were vacant. We went to a bar with friends and I noticed that when anyone spoke to him he mostly just nodded and smiled.

"You have to go to sleep," I said to him quietly.

"I know," he said.

The next morning he went to see a doctor, who prescribed sleeping pills. We walked together into town to fill the prescription. We were both happy and relaxed. His problem would soon be solved. He went to sleep that night, but I did not.

Five days before P.J. was supposed to arrive, he told me that he was interested in one of our friends, whom I'll call Kristin. She seemed to be interested in return. Did I think that was okay? Previously we had agreed that friends were off limits. But we had five days left and I told him to go for it. The next day when he called and told me that he had slept with Kristin, I was relieved. My guilt had taken on a physical quality. Every day in the late afternoon, a burning sensation had crept up my esophagus and spread outward through my chest. "My chest is on fire," I told Michael. "It's heartburn," he said, offering me an antacid.

My hotel room was a mess, the bed unmade, dirty clothes and drafts everywhere. In the midst of my own marital maelstrom, I couldn't think clearly about Barbara's, and to cope I wrote meandering drafts as quickly as possible and scattered them around the room in the hopes that clarity might suddenly appear.

This was not like me. Messy rooms normally drove me crazy. The sight of a countertop heaped with books, water bottles, old receipts, and computer cords made me feel as though my life had become unhinged. I admired people who seemed unfazed by their messy houses. They were more liberated, their internal worlds not so easily shaken by their physical surroundings. But now, with my life in chaos, there was too much else to worry about.

My relief at P.J.'s news disgusted me. As I got off the phone with him, I wondered what kind of person is relieved when her husband announces he is sleeping with someone else.

Occasionally, I would recall the feeling of loving just P.J. and feel a pang of longing. I missed the uncomplicated, urgent love that comes at the beginning of relationships, when all your attention lands like a laser beam on one person. Your work doesn't matter, trivial disagreements with friends or family members are forgotten, all is blown away by the blunt force of that new, singular love. It reminded me of the beginning of *Anna Karenina*, when Levin falls in love with Kitty: "for him all the girls in the world were divided into two sorts: one sort was all the girls in the world except her . . . the other sort was her alone."

"You don't love me the way I love you," Michael would say. "This is quit-your-job kind of love, sell-your-house kind of love, move-anywhere kind of love." He was right. My love was divided.

I told Taylor that I needed to run alone that day and laced up my running shoes. I raced down the hill by the Bow River and made my way to a quiet road that overlooked a lake and a mountain. I picked up speed, feeling electrified and miserable. A pack of firs lined the road. As I came around the bend, an enormous elk stood in the path, its antlers raised skyward. It looked at me indifferently and turned back to grazing. I stopped, struck by its imposing muscular frame, and thought I could see its nostrils flare as it breathed. I tiptoed around it in thrall, giving it a wide berth, and made my way farther down the road, feeling my strength return as blood beat in my temples. My feet seemed to fly over the pavement, and the cool mountain air rushed over my skin. A woman alone. A lone traveler. A lone wolf. Maybe this was how I was supposed to be. I broke into a sprint, my blood pounding through my body, my chest heaving, and all thoughts were driven out.

After my run, I had lunch with one of the program's faculty to discuss my draft. Charlotte is svelte and strikingly beautiful. She has alert green eyes and the serene expression of a meditation guru but is too sharp to speak in New Age tropes. We ate salads in front of the dining hall's floor-to-ceiling plate-glass windows, and suddenly anxious for a disinterested party to confide in, I told her about my marital experiment. Her eyebrows raised and a subtle smile spread over her face.

Charlotte and I discussed whether I should write about my open marriage. She reminded me that there were ways to allude to things without explicitly addressing them, ways to avoid having to fully open myself to the scrutinizing eye of a reader. "You can't lie, but you don't owe anyone everything," she said. But I knew that I would write this story explicitly. I would omit certain details, but I didn't want to hide behind allusions and coy insinuations. I wanted to walk loudly on the page and pay no heed to those with delicate sensibilities. I wanted to be this more fearless me forever. Writing about that self would preserve her in print. Is this not also what Barbara had done? I wondered if her obsessive recording of her own adventures was a way to ward off unwanted lives, lives she might also have been attracted to. She'd had a taste of her ideal self at sea and sought to enshrine that self on the page. Should her incoherent, ephemeral self ever disappoint over the course of her life, the self she had created in black type would be there—simpler, better.

I told Charlotte I would consider what she was saying, but that, more pressingly, I didn't know how to end my draft. She gazed at me with that cool, serene smile. "That's because the end hasn't happened yet."

FIFTEEN

The night before P.J. arrived, I couldn't sleep. I realized it was possible that he might not show up. It would be highly out of character, yes, but suddenly everything seemed possible. P.J. and I hadn't spoken much over the last couple of days; he had spent them with Kristin. I had been focused on Michael and on turning in my draft, and there had been a steady stream of social events as the residency wrapped up. Lying in the dark I imagined P.J.'s and Kristin's bodies entangled, limb over limb in our bed. I felt nothing except for a vague hope that things wouldn't be awkward between Kristin and me.

What was P.J. thinking? Was he dreading seeing me? Was he in love with Kristin? I had for so many years inhabited P.J.'s brain. I felt I understood every glance and gesture and its corresponding thought. At dinner parties, I knew the look that meant someone had just said something appalling, after which he would feel compelled to disagree with a polite, "Well, but . . ." I knew the flash of animation that came across his face when something excited him. We can never truly know what someone else is thinking, but I fancied we had, at moments at least, gotten pretty close.

But now, flailing around in my bed, thinking that if I just fluffed my pillow one more time or tightened the blinds, then I might get to sleep, P.J. was a total mystery to me. And while I was desperate to know what he was thinking, I also wondered if there wasn't something stifling about so fully inhabiting someone else's mental space.

I recalled a nature documentary in which a fungus invades an ant's body. The fungus inside the ant causes it to climb to a particular height on a plant. Once there, the fungus emerges from the top of the ant's head in a bulbous, alien protrusion and releases its spores, the ant's corpse now having served its purpose. Had P.J. and I burrowed into each other's minds, and in so doing, devoured one another? It suddenly seemed that all the things that were beautiful about being married—the finishing of each other's sentences, the communicating without words, the feeling of being known—could be self-annihilating.

In those early-morning hours when everything dangerous seems certain to happen, I could imagine in precise detail what it would be like for P.J. not to come to Banff, and I knew that this possibility was really what was keeping me up. I could see myself standing on the curb in front of the reception building, straining to see inside each car that could possibly be his. The next day, he would—or wouldn't—walk back into my life, and I couldn't decide which possibility scared me more.

The next day I stood at the entrance to the arts center in my black dress. All the residents would be giving a reading later that night, and P.J. would be arriving just in time for it. He texted to say he had gotten on the plane but that his phone was dying. He was renting a car in Calgary, which was about an hour and a half away. He hadn't slept the night before and had waited until the last possible minute to pack.

I arrived fifteen minutes early. I brought a book, but I couldn't read. I didn't know what the rental car looked like, so I craned my neck and peered into every passing car. Fifteen minutes went by, then thirty. I paced anxiously. When he was forty-five minutes late, I began to really worry. I imagined him barreling down the highway, windows rolled down, the wind blowing through his hair. All our camping gear was in the back, and as the mountains rose up before him, he might think to himself, fuck it, and turn off the highway and drive out into the majestic scenery. A man alone with nothing but the sky, the pine trees, and the Rocky Mountains. Could I really blame him? P.J. had never been the type to ditch and run, but each passing minute intensified my paranoia. What if everything I understood about him had changed? I thought with irritation about how he hadn't charged his phone, hadn't packed until the last minute, and wondered if our experiment had turned him into some kind of irresponsible man-child. I wondered if, on some level, I didn't want him to come because then I might see that the spark that animated our marriage was gone.

A prickly sensation of shame crept all over my skin. I imagined walking up to the podium to take my turn. I would be reading the scene where Barbara vanished, and P.J.'s empty chair in the second row would suddenly seem enormous, somehow larger than the other seats in the auditorium, its emptiness a potent rebuke. The draft I had turned in was dishonest. "Let us see the cracks in your marriage," one of the program's editors urged me. One night, as I slept beside Michael, I dreamed the editor was in the room, standing over our bed, and said, "Ah, now I see the cracks in your marriage."

Another car drove into the entrance and I looked frantically inside. It was a middle-aged man with a goatee. A pickup truck followed, and I peered into that too, though it was hard to imagine P.J. renting a pickup truck. The sound check was at five. I would wait until 4:52, I decided, then I would run to the auditorium and quickly down a glass of white wine. Further up the drive, closer to the reception area, which was partially concealed by a row of pine trees, I saw another woman from my program, Alex, also waiting for her husband. His car pulled up and he jumped out. They locked in a long embrace and kissed. I felt a flush of envy.

Alex and her husband came over and I pretended to be surprised to see them. I introduced myself to her husband, Jeremy.

"Are you waiting for P.J.?" Alex asked.

"Yeah," I tried to say nonchalantly. "He's a little late, but should be here any minute."

"Oh, what does he look like?" Jeremy asked.

How nice to have a helpful husband, I thought. How nice to rush into someone's arms and then have him be cheerful and helpful to your friends. I showed Jeremy a picture. "If you need to go to the sound check, I can keep an eye out for him," he said.

"I'll wait a few more minutes, but thanks."

"There was a lot of traffic between here and Calgary," he said. "There was an accident or something."

"Oh, yeah, that's probably it," I said, and then paused. "What did the car look like? The one in the accident, I mean."

"Not sure," Jeremy said.

It would serve me right, I thought. How greedy I had been,

wanting not just his love but more. I looked at my watch. It was 4:52. I had to go. I walked into the reception area and told the man at the desk that P.J. should be coming soon and asked if he could tell him to go to the auditorium.

As I left the reception area I saw a white sedan parked nearby. P.J. got out of the driver's seat.

"Hi, stranger," he said.

SIXTEEN

There is another, much sadder reading of Barbara's disappearance. She was not some masterful magician orchestrating her own vanishing act. Magicians don't vanish, they make their assistants vanish. A beautiful woman steps into a box and the magician makes her disappear. She is the stage prop. He decides when she will be seen and when she won't. He can bring her into being. He can also make her nothing. The audience claps.

I had told myself that Barbara's disappearance had given her power—the power to hold people in thrall, to leave them wondering. It was a way to remain on people's minds. Nick would have wondered for the rest of his life. But from another perspective, the vanishing woman is a trope and not a very empowering one at all. I could think of dozens of stories about enigmatic disappearing women. In this fantasy, I saw a troubling unwillingness to take women as they actually are.

Once, sitting in the Columbia archives, I had come across a letter in which Barbara had expressed disapproval of mixed-race marriages. I wanted her to be more progressive than that. The vanished woman is perfect because she is whoever we want her to be. She doesn't grow old, or fat, or ugly; she doesn't say things we don't like. She is frozen, no longer her own, but ours.

Would I have written about Barbara if she hadn't disappeared?

Probably not. It was the metamorphosis from woman to enigma that captivated me most. I was using her story for my own purposes. I was not so much telling her story as appropriating it.

I told myself that my intentions were better than that, that I was trying to reverse the process, to unvanish her. I believed she was the magician and I wanted proof that it was true. But even in that more flattering scenario, I had still cast myself in the role of explorer, invader, planting my flag in her unknown lands.

So which was it? Was she the stage prop or the magician? When we date someone we say we are "seeing" them. *I'm seeing someone from work.* To be loved is to be seen, noticed, selected from the masses of humanity as someone remarkable and worthy of special attention. Barbara's husband fell out of love with her and wanted to be with someone else. To be fallen out of love with is to be rendered invisible. *I'm seeing someone else now. I'm not seeing you anymore.*

"This isn't a story about the vanishing of a woman," Michael said to me one day. "This is a story about the vanishing of love."

I had the feeling we weren't talking about Barbara anymore.

P.J. and Michael met at the reception after the reading. At the cocktail event, surrounded by faculty, friends, and the audience, they shook hands. I believe they spoke about baseball, which baffled me as I have never known P.J. to speak about baseball. Both were uncomfortable but tried to seem friendly and at ease, to unweird our impossibly weird situation. I moved uneasily between them, unsure who needed my reassurances more. I found P.J.'s upbeat demeanor unconvincing, his excessive ease masking his discomfort in an awkward and humiliating situation. Michael was less gregarious than usual, but he didn't seem unhappy. He had told me the night before that he valued our time together, and that it had been an important lesson in learning how to love without possession. I had felt relieved. Now at the event I told myself the meeting was going well. Michael said he needed a smoke and P.J. joined him. At a distance, through the plate-glass window, I watched them talk outside. Someone might see them, I thought, and think they are great friends. I felt like a nervous pet owner. *Look how well they are playing!*

P.J. was exhausted from not sleeping and from the jet lag, and I was exhausted from stress, so eventually, we excused ourselves and went back to my hotel room. We turned on the last two episodes of a show we had obsessively watched together in New York. In the penultimate episode, one of the main characters is diagnosed with terminal cancer. I didn't feel particularly attached to that character—in fact, I didn't really like her—but I cried my heart out, with a chest-heaving kind of sob that I hadn't experienced since childhood. I cried so long and hard that when I got up the next morning and looked in the mirror, I thought my face had exploded. My eyes were swollen and red. I ran my face under the icy faucet water and checked again. I looked the same. I considered that maybe I had done myself permanent damage. P.J. did not seem particularly alarmed by the state of my face. He rolled over and went back to sleep. I took note and raced downstairs to grab a coffee and prepare for one final meeting, hoping I wouldn't run into anyone I knew. I immediately bumped into Michael in the hallway. He looked stricken when he saw me.

"Oh, my god, what happened?" he asked.

"I think I broke my face," I said.

I knew then that I was in big trouble. When P.J. had appeared, he had given voice to my worst fear. We were strangers. Michael, with his endless reassurances of devotion and deep concern, was suddenly the one who understood me.

"Is there any way I can talk to you alone later?" he asked.

Yes, I said. Of course. I could meet with whomever I wanted. I was a free person. I suggested the wine bar nearby. But even as I reassured myself of my freedom, it didn't quite feel true anymore—that phase was over.

I arrived at the wine bar early.

"We will need a bottle," I told the waiter.

I had told P.J. I would just be an hour, concerned that more than that might alarm him. Having totally abdicated the conventional rules of marriage, I created new rules. I could meet with Michael but only for an hour. I assured myself that this made total sense because talking to Michael would give me "closure." I'm going to end things on a good note, I told myself as I sat at the bar. I'm making the transition to friendship. I could feel myself lying.

Seeking closure was an excuse to act on the desires of what I began to call "the irrational love brain." The irrational love brain wants what it wants, which is to be near the person it loves. It pays no heed to its own well-being, work, sleep, or the well-being of others. I thought back on the millions of excuses I had heard friends make over the years to be near the people they loved impossibly. One friend applied for a job at her ex's company, arguing that she wanted to prove to herself that she no longer cared and could work near him. "That's insane," I told her. It is so easy to recognize the garbled thinking and willful self-deception of the irrational love brain when you are not lost in its fog. "If you really didn't care, you would work at literally any other company," I told her. No, she said, it had to be that one. Another friend kept having one last dinner, then another one, and no, really, this time was the last dinner, hoping the person he loved but could not be with would say the magic words that would release him from the animal devotion that was gnawing at him—or was it giving him life? He wasn't sure. Then he could move on, he said. I suspected that really the last dinner was a last-ditch effort to change her mind.

The irrational love brain doesn't want to move on. The "last" meeting is always another opportunity to catapult yourself back into the love frenzy that you now need in order to eat, sleep, work—live. Because if you really want to be released from love, the only surefire way that I've ever seen is total banishment. There are no more coffees, no late-night texting. It requires blocking all social media accounts. Sometimes it involves moving to the other side of the world so that you don't hang out at that bar she likes, hoping for a chance encounter. That's how you make your love vanish.

My irrational love brain argued in favor of a "new" kind of relationship in which Michael and I would continue to love each other even though we weren't together. I convinced myself that this arrangement would hurt no one, but be a kind of uberfriend-ship that defied conventional labels. Michael's irrational love brain told him that if he waited, I would come.

As the wine arrived, a friend walked through the door. I felt a flash of dread when she sat down and joined me. I could not let this happen. My last meeting with Michael could not turn into a small-talk triangle. I felt the old vinelike powerlessness creeping over me, the inability to say no, the fear that if I told someone what I truly wanted, they wouldn't like me anymore.

But now I saw that I had wandered through my life acting terribly put-upon. People made me do things, I claimed. Sitting at the bar, I saw with clarity that I had blamed not achieving the things I wanted on the intrusions of others, because that was easier than blaming myself. If I didn't write books, if I didn't have private conversations when I wanted them, I had no one to blame but myself.

"I'm meeting Michael," I said after greeting my friend. "And I need to talk to him alone about something sort of sensitive." I was surprised and pleased by the strength I heard in my own voice. She said of course she understood. It had been that easy. I had spent the last month enjoying the power of saying yes, but now I realized that saying no was revolutionary. I had the power to be disappointing, and with that power I could craft a life.

Michael seemed disappointed when he saw the woman, but she quickly got up.

"I told her she couldn't stay," I said proudly. "I told her I needed to talk to you alone." Did he realize that I hadn't always been this way? I imagined myself as some kind of Aztec queen standing on top of a volcano, commanding these other me's, paltry me's in plain white tunics, to jump into the fire. *Let them burn!* I thought.

"Let's sit over there," I said, gesturing to a more private corner of the bar. I led him to the other table and when we sat down, he started to cry.

P.J. and I stayed in Banff for three days after everyone left. We had planned to camp in the Canadian Rockies for two weeks, but a viscous lethargy had settled in on us. Packing our bags, grocery shopping, and finding a campsite seemed to require Herculean effort, so we delayed.

But staying was a terrible idea. A particular street corner, a stairwell, or even just passing by the grocery store conjured memories of Michael. As P.J. and I walked around downtown Banff, I avoided the little white cottage with the hydrangea and rain boots by the front door. When we passed by the Mexican restaurant where Michael had touched my foot under the table, I felt a pang of longing, quickly followed by guilt. P.J. was unwittingly taking a tour of my other life.

P.J. and I had had a special language and nicknames, but now we didn't use them and I hardly noticed. It was Michael's movements, his manner of talking, that pressed on me with more urgency, even though he wasn't there. He was a ghost haunting my marriage and P.J. wasn't even trying to banish him or to win me back. Our marriage felt as though someone had walked into a room, opened all the windows, and let something essential flutter out.

In our hotel room, when P.J. put on a song I didn't recognize I wondered if Kristin had introduced him to it. Their relationship hadn't been as involved. They hadn't had very much time together. She seemed to accept the rules of the arrangement, never pressuring P.J. for more than he was willing to give. She had even sent me a note asking if everything was all right.

Still, I worried that P.J. and I had allowed ourselves a touch of something that might bloom into something dangerous. He wouldn't have to smell her morning breath, or see her in a truly foul mood. I would never have to navigate filing joint taxes with Michael. Not knowing how these relationships would bear out over time, we risked idealizing them.

When we finally left Banff to go camping, it was raining. We stopped in a coffee shop near the highway. I watched the downpour transform everything around me into gray dullness. The Icefields Parkway is a 140-mile road that threads through mountainous wilderness. It begins at the Trans-Canada Highway going over the Saskatchewan River Crossing, following the Continental Divide to Jasper, which lies on the eastern edge of Alberta, near British Columbia. It is flanked on either side by vast stretches of evergreen trees, striking glacier-melt lakes, and rugged rock faces.

We had a campsite map and decided to make our way up the parkway until it stopped raining. P.J. drove and I sat next to him in the passenger's seat, fiddling with the radio until we lost reception. Outside the car window, the clouds broke and afternoon sunlight filtered through the trees. Enjoy this, I instructed myself. One day you will not be here and you'll wish you had appreciated it more. But I felt a deadening malaise.

It occurred to me that maybe it was a bad time to be on an intensely isolated vacation. There would be no phones or televisions to distract us, no friends to meet for coffee, just the sounds of cicadas, trickling creeks, and whatever we said to each other. I wanted to drown out the chatter in my head. I told myself that this was better. We will have to face our problems directly, I thought. We will emerge from the wilderness in two weeks either stronger or irrevocably broken.

We stopped first at Mosquito Creek, tired and hungry, hoping that it had been inaccurately named. As we unloaded the car, we saw families camping nearby. This seemed a good sign. Parents wouldn't take their children to a mosquito-infested campsite. We pitched our tent, opened a can of sardines and ate them on sliced bread, and quickly discovered that Mosquito Creek is aptly named. Its mosquitoes were capable of biting through material as thick as jeans. All evening I heard their high-pitched, devilish whine around my ears. I wore my hoodie cinched up around my face, leaving only a small hole for my eyes and nose, and still I constantly discovered new bites. "Let's get out of here," I said the next morning when we woke up. "This place is miserable."

The next campground was no better. We pitched our tent as far from the river as possible, hoping to steer clear of mosquitoes. But on the way to a hike, with my feet on the car's dashboard, I counted sixty-seven bites. That night we ate peanut butter sandwiches and drank whiskey straight from the bottle by the campfire. This is the low point, I told myself. From here, it will get better.

I missed the feeling of missing P.J. and found I couldn't conjure my former affection for him. Sometimes as he packed his backpack or hammered the stakes of the tent into the ground I would be struck by how handsome he was. I noticed the thoughtful expression he made when he focused on something, his dark angular features, his sensitive eyes. But the feelings attached to these observations were locked away somewhere. Something dark was moving through the empty space in our marriage, and I was scared this state would last forever.

Whereas previously P.J. was always circling back on what he'd said, interrupting himself with a new thought, now he chose his words carefully, occasionally freezing in midsentence. The more I tried to lure warmth and feeling back to our relationship, the more elusive those things became. I worried that love was like a body, that once those nerves are dead, there is no reviving them.

"Be warm to me!" I said as we gathered firewood by the river near our campsite.

"I'm trying," he said.

At other times, I would notice the freckle on his upper lip, or the way his hair matted when he took off his baseball cap, and feel a surge of affection—followed by relief. Oh good, it—whatever it was—was not gone. He would apologize for his coldness and kiss the top of my head and pull me into his arms. But just as soon as I had acknowledged the flicker of feeling, it vanished, leaving me to wonder if it had been a mirage conjured in my desperation.

At night, I lied to myself in my journal. I acknowledged the indifference, but I also wrote lines like, "I feel peaceful about everything that has happened," and "All is good here." Not true. My new baseline was frenzied despair. I had no idea what was going on, wasn't sure how I felt, what I wanted, or what P.J. wanted. I thought I could write myself into a better state of mind, that I could will myself out of indifference. I recalled the postcard Barbara had sent from the bus stop in Kansas. "Am really feeling O.K. and well under control!" Only then did I understand what a total load of bullshit that was, how much a major life upheaval can turn you into a self-deception machine, and how essential this was to making the hours bearable. The pin that had anchored me to my life had slipped away. Or had I deliberately yanked it out?

SEVENTEEN

Nick never told anyone what they discussed the night Barbara vanished. That final conversation—or was it a fight?—was the last time anyone who knew Barbara interacted with her, as far as I knew. Perhaps he told her that the relationship with Anne was serious—or even that he intended to leave her to be with Anne.

What was abundantly clear was that there was much more at stake than a marriage. Barbara's whole identity was unraveling—though perhaps this is always the case at the end of a marriage. She had become the kind of person she had always despised, pleading with her husband to stay, trying to win him back with housekeeping. She had always seen herself as the elusive one, the adventurous one, the one being chased—not the one doing the chasing. But here she was for the second time in her life advocating for the opposite of running away: preserving a home. She must have noticed the inconsistency of her position, the person she wanted to be clashing uncomfortably with the person she was becoming. Leaving rather than being left was a way to reclaim her bolder, more adventurous identity.

I wondered if, rather than striking out entirely on her own, she might have gone to someone for affirmation—someone who would see her as she wanted to be seen. Barbara's friends and family kept mentioning one such person. Alice had tried to track him down with no success.

Before Nick, Barbara had been in love with another man. His name was Ed Anderson, though everyone called him Anderson, and in most of her letters, Barbara referred to him simply as A. He was the sailor she had broken up with to be with Nick. She had met him while traveling from Honolulu to Washington aboard the *Vigilant,* where he was working as the ship's second mate. An account of their meeting can be found in Helen's book *Stars to Steer By.* When Barbara first saw Anderson he was sitting at the boat's stern at dusk, just beginning his night watch. He seemed to be a part of the ship, distinct from the dusk only by the orange glow of his cigarette. As Barbara and her mother approached, they had the sense they were intruding, that he was a man who preferred to be alone.

"Don't go away on my account," he said, sensing their retreat.

He told Barbara that he liked the night watch because it was quiet. "Not so much talk going on."

He asked if Barbara was disappointed by life at sea.

She said no, quite the opposite. "This is what I've wanted for three years," she said. "A ship can't disappoint, the way people can."

"Strange," Anderson replied, "to find someone who says the things I think myself. . . . Yes, here you're safe from people and disappointment."

They fell in love. He was much older—around twenty-five to her fifteen. They talked about literature, quoting John Masefield's poem "Sea-Fever" to each other. He was tall with a broad frame, prone to moody ruminations about the failings of civilization and the futility of life. Barbara was drawn to his darkness. His gritty, working-class life was romantic to her, in part no doubt because she had never had to live it. Anderson knew better, reminding her that such harshness could wear you away. He had hacked his way through Arctic ice sheets and sailed all over the Pacific, and though he complained about it, it seemed the only life for him.

They sailed together for a month before they arrived in Washington State. By then it was July. Barbara and Helen stayed with him for a week aboard the empty ship docked at Gray's Harbor. The three of them would have cherry and ice cream parties on the empty deck and then walk in the forest to eat wild berries. The young lovers separated at the end of the week when Helen sent Barbara to guardians in California. Shortly thereafter Barbara ran away. Could Anderson have been the "we" that Barbara referenced in her runaway letter to her mother?

The relationship continued when Barbara and her mother moved to New York. She and Anderson exchanged letters religiously. Anderson comforted her during those dreadful days when she worked the office job and felt everything she had dreamed of—the sea, an adventurous life—slipping from her grasp.

"One could starve to death on an enviable job—for mountain wind, for stars among pine trees, or the call of a wood-thrush to his mate," she wrote. The typewriter that had once set her imagination free now became an instrument of menial labor. Going from being the darling child genius novelist to a secretary must have been a blow. "Oh, oh," she wrote to Alice, "in N.Y. the moths feed on the wings of your soul."

"Anderson is marvellous," she wrote. "Honestly, I don't see how I could possibly get along without his twice—and sometimes thrice—weekly communications: all done in the best Anderso-nian manner, and never less than two pages in length. He is— a rock." He was loyal and supportive, everything she felt her father was not. His letters reminded her that their life at sea was not so far off.

When she came home from the office, she worked on *Lost Island*. The love interest in *Lost Island,* Davidson, was based on Anderson. In the book, Davidson represents an escape from a humdrum office job, the promise of a life of adventure. Barbara's dread about her life in New York, her desire for something that would make her heart thump in her chest, was steadily building. At night, she tossed and turned for hours. She had been at the job for nearly two years when she met Nick and began hatching her Appalachian Trail plan.

Anderson's role in her life was mostly symbolic. Over those two years, they hardly saw each other and one of his letters reveals they never had sex. To Barbara, Anderson was more of an idea than an actual person.

In time, the long distance began to wear on them. Barbara wondered about his constantly roving, seafaring life. She wrote to Alice, "His life is odd and stern—verging on tragic, at times." In July, she began her hike on the Appalachian Trail with Nick. She broke it off with Anderson in a letter soon after. Anderson wrote back calling Nick "Dartmouth," a slur perhaps meant to remind her that Ivy boys are not true adventurers. "You are life and adventure itself," he wrote, "and you're completely wasted on anything else."

"You see Bar, I knew ever so long ago that you wanted more than just one life; the 'restlessly sampling' you speak of was too obvious, even for a man in love to avoid seeing." He went on to advise her: "All of us wish more than one life and the great art of it is in blending the many lives into one." A life with Nick, a well-educated man, offered more security, but Anderson knew security wasn't really what she was after. She needed a roving life, like the one she would have with him. She wouldn't have to pick an island if she stayed with him. She could have all the islands. He signed his letter, "I want you, A."

Barbara continued to think of Anderson after her marriage to Nick, dedicating her novel *Lost Island* to him even though she finished it the year she got married. In 1935, a year after she got married, she wrote to him. They had not exchanged words in over two years, since she hiked the Appalachian Trail with Nick. Now settled in Brookline, trapped in another office job with a long married life before her, she was feeling a little restless, though it's not clear she told him this. Anderson wrote a long letter back. "I think I'm the biggest fool in creation. Whatever it was went wrong, I know I was almost entirely to blame." He wasn't married and was still working the same job. "As for escape, I've learned a lot about that too. There is no escape for those who think they need it." Then in the middle of the letter, without warning, he wrote, "I'm still in love with you."

Anderson's devotion may have been appealing in the face of Nick's infidelity. He had made a prediction about Nick when Barbara wrote to him from the trail to say she was choosing Nick over him: "I do not say you may tire, but what of him, may he not. With me it might be harder, but more lasting, I know." From the beginning, Anderson had set up a dichotomy between himself and Nick. Anderson was offering a life of adventure. Nick was offering a life of stability. Anderson had implored her, "Put on your cap and coat and come West."

She wouldn't have necessarily gone to him for romance when she left in 1939—it had been four years since their last exchange the year after her marriage—but perhaps it would have been comforting to stop by and see him, to be in the presence of someone who professed his devotion and thought of her "as life and adventure itself."

"Happiness, contentment, security, bah, give me freedom," Anderson had written. He was a good person to know if you were trying to get out of town. He knew sailors and routes all over the world and would be eager to help. He offered the possibility of a plot twist in her life that was more to her liking. She wasn't a discarded wife: she was an adventurer. What if she had turned personal loss into an opportunity? I decided that when I got back to New York, I would look for Anderson.

A few days into our trip, P.J. and I went to a campground thirty minutes from Jasper. We were tired of eating out of cans, and the thought of a proper shower was too enticing to resist. Our new campsite was surrounded by evergreens in a wide valley. We could hear the Snaring River rushing gently while we fell asleep. At night, by the light of our headlamps, we talked for hours. We went to a bakery in the morning and drank hot coffee. In the bakery parking lot we bought weed from some sixty-year-old hippies who were worried that we were the police. "We're not the police. Are you the police?" we asked, knowing full well that they were not.

That afternoon, we went on a long trail run to Jacques Lake, occasionally calling out or clapping as we ran along the overgrown trail to avoid startling the bears, because a ranger had told us that was how people get eaten. We arrived at the lake and found a moose and its baby grazing along the edge. We ate peanut butter straight from the jar as we watched the moose. I had become a relationship barometer, constantly evaluating the state of our marriage. I decided things were so-so, but trending in the right direction. Occasionally we talked about whether our arrangement would continue. We agreed that it was hard to conceive of being with other people right then. We were both so raw. But we didn't want to decide the issue firmly. Imagining the future was impossible when just navigating the moment felt overwhelming. There was only now, and in many ways this was a relief.

The next morning, I opened the flaps of our tent to find P.J. sitting by our campfire scribbling in his journal. When I asked him what he was doing he said he was calculating the number of days we had both spent with other people and trying to determine if he cared that there was a disparity in our experiences. He seemed sheepish, but I was furious. I felt I had been given permission to act without guilt, only to be punished later. We'd had fun the past few days, trail running and enjoying the mosquito-free campsite. I couldn't bear the thought of backtracking. All the talking, all the problem solving had sapped me of energy. I looked around at the campsite and decided that I needed to be alone. I had been tied to P.J.'s side for days and I missed my freedom, the carefree way that a person on her own can get up and go whenever she decides she needs to.

"We need a few hours apart," I said. I told him I would take the car into town for coffee and a run. I wanted to be the one to go away, to be on the move. P.J. looked a little worried and sad, but he agreed. If I left, there would be clarity, I thought. And maybe I would miss him.

A long, straight road leads out of the Snaring River Campground, up a wide-open plane of prairie grass and rocky, dry earth. The morning light cast shadows on Pyramid Mountain and the air was sharp and clear. I rolled down the windows, feeling relieved to be alone. I went to a little coffee shop in town. Families on vacation passed by in groups, and I sat quietly at the sidewalk café, feeling unencumbered for the first time in weeks.

When I finished my coffee, I jogged on the Pyramid Bench Trail that runs behind town. I felt lighter and thought of P.J. He always worried when I ran on trails by myself. I was ready to go back, to assure him that I hadn't been killed.

When I found him back at the campsite, I felt a surge of affection. We hugged, apologizing for the morning, and made plans to eat pizza in town that night. Something that had been blocked between us had come loose and we talked easily and eagerly now. We smoked the weed we had bought from the old hippies and went to dinner. He gripped my arms and told me I looked beautiful.

"We made such a mess," I said to him and he agreed. We shook our heads, smiling. "There were times when I didn't know who I was, when I felt like I didn't have anything to hang on to," he said.

Michael had called our marital arrangement an "experiment in chaos," and he was right. The pain was not just an unfortunate side effect, but part of the goal. Sometimes pain is preferable to blankness. There is something electric and clarifying about hurting, something intoxicating about experiencing everything on the spectrum from agony to exaltation.

In his memoir on addiction, David Carr wrote, "When there is no edge, we make our own." He made his edge with cocaine. By his own admission, he was making trouble where there didn't have to be any, and so was I. But I also saw destruction's revolutionary potential. From the mess you make of your life, you could build something new and it might be better—*you* might be better.

A particularly shrewd friend asked me once if I envied Barbara. Of course the answer on some level was yes. To seize your life and abruptly change course—to disappear—that seemed like real power. The saddest way to leave is to fade, to stay too long at a party when the hosts are yawning and want you to leave. There was something alluring to me about premature departures, about people wanting and missing you, or not really ever having you.

But Barbara's spectacular exit hadn't saved her from fading. Her disappearance hadn't inspired a mad search. So much of *The House Without Windows* had been about the chase, but when Barbara disappeared in real life, the chase was strangely half-hearted and lacking in urgency. There were no dogs sniffing in the woods, no headlines in broadsheets. Her employers presumably hired a new secretary. The clothes that hung in her closet were perhaps loaded into boxes and given away—or were they thrown away? Her husband eventually divorced her in absentia and remarried. Part of the appeal of vanishing is the expectation that you will be longed for. But you can't predict or control how people will react. Maybe they won't miss you.

"The worst is over, right?" I asked P.J.

"I think so," he said.

The next day, I got an e-mail from Michael. P.J. and I had plans to go backcountry camping for three days in British Columbia before returning to New York. "Know this," Michael's e-mail read, "there's a man on the other side of the country who loves you." He said he wanted to visit when we got back.

EIGHTEEN

I wasn't the only person who considered that Barbara might have contacted Anderson after leaving. Helen had asked Alice if she had heard from him. Alice reported that after Barbara's disappearance, she had written him a letter, but the letter had been returned to sender.

A few years earlier, I had contacted Barbara's nephew Stefan—Margaret and Wilson's grandson. He knew more about Barbara than anyone else I had come across. He had typed up nearly all her letters and had carefully arranged and annotated them in a book he was calling *Barbara Newhall Follett: A Life in Letters*, which he had self-published. We met in Somerville, near Brookline, shortly after I had visited Barbara's house and the Brookline police station to examine their files on Barbara, which were minimal. Stefan has an intense, serious manner, and his grandfather's fastidious attention to grammatical precision, occasionally correcting errors in my e-mails. Despite this well-meaning curmudgeonliness, something about him moved me. Maybe it was his total devotion to Barbara's story, or a sort of wistful restlessness that he gave off. His careful cataloging of the work of the aunt he had never met seemed an attempt to tame something within himself, a quality I related to. In a loud, warehouse-style coffee shop, I asked him what he thought had happened to Barbara. The first thing he said was that maybe she had run off with Anderson. This was, of course, the outcome we both wanted to believe. But it was also true that in the tracking down of old friends after Barbara disappeared, Anderson was the only one unaccounted for.

P.J. and I returned to New York at the end of August. The place felt at once familiar, but also strange. We had been through a tumultuous, transformational summer—how could everything just be the same as when we had left? Going to the same restaurants, walking down the same streets, picking up our old routines was comforting, but it also highlighted the ways in which we had changed. I had been so sure that the two weeks in the woods would smooth things out between us. But in many ways, being back at home among our friends and belongings left me feeling more confused than ever. Nothing was resolved.

There were several factors complicating my search for Anderson. For one thing, I wasn't entirely sure what his first name was. In letters, he was referred to only as "Anderson." In Barbara's mother's book, he was "the second mate." Online I found a manifest from the ship where he worked for years, the *C.S. Holmes*. He was listed as "E. Anderson." Going through Barbara's letters, I found one from Gordon Campbell, a fellow shipmate, who had sailed with them. He referred to Anderson as "Ed." It was still a common name, but it narrowed the field a bit. He could be Edward, Edmund, or Edgar. Or Edwin. According to the manifest, he was American, which helped a little because many of the other Andersons or Andersens I came across were Swedish.

The other available details were paltry. I knew he was tall—six foot two, according to the ship manifest. I knew from letters that he was roughly ten years older than Barbara, which meant he was most likely born between 1903 and 1905. I knew that according to his last letter, he had lived in Seattle for at least five years and that as of 1935 he wasn't married. But that was it. I didn't know what state he was from. I didn't know what he looked like. There was no mention of family or any kind of personal history in his letters. In the archives at Columbia, I came across a picture of him on the deck of a small ship in the Arctic. He was leaning against the mast, his face entirely obscured by shadow. He was a shade, a ghost. It reminded me of Helen's description of him as barely distinguishable from the ship's darkness as he sat on deck. The murkiness of the details only made me want to find him more. And finding him would offer a clue about Barbara. At the very least I hoped to rule out the possibility that she had gone to him.

I found a letter from a shipmate of his, who had written to Barbara in 1934 and reported that Anderson had told him that he was going to do two more stints with the *C.S. Holmes,* then he would build his own boat and settle in Alaska, where he would hunt and fish. I decided to start my search in Alaska and Seattle, his last known address. I added Hawaii because I knew Anderson had sailed there. Alaska and Hawaii were not states at the time, and careful international travel records were kept of crew and passengers. But the name on the *C.S. Holmes* manifest was the only one I could find that was definitively him. I found hundreds of other Andersons in the online database of ship manifests, but there was always a way to rule them out as not "my" Anderson. They were too short, not born in America, too young, too old, or held positions Anderson likely wouldn't have held, like cook, since he had previously been a second, then first mate. I saved records of the ones who were close, figuring it was possible that someone made a mistake with the birth date or nationality. When nothing turned up under Ed Anderson, I began searching E. Anderson, then just Anderson. No matches.

I looked up Anderson's last known address, on Ewing Street in Seattle, and discovered that it currently belonged to Foss Maritime Company, a private shipping company specializing in tugboat cargo. The name sounded familiar. I looked through my notes and discovered an article that mentioned that Foss owned the *C.S. Holmes*. The company Anderson had worked for was still in operation.

I called them and a woman answered the phone. I awkwardly explained why I was calling: I was trying to find information about a sailor who had worked for them some eighty-odd years ago because I was looking for his former girlfriend, who had vanished, and I thought maybe she had run off with him. "Oh, that's interesting!" the woman said. She offered to connect me to a man who had worked at Foss "forever" and was their "unofficial resident historian." The man picked up. I was disappointed that he didn't sound decrepitly old, and realized that I had briefly entertained a fantasy that he had been working at Foss for so long that he might have crossed paths with Anderson. I told the man the same story. Had Anderson continued to work for Foss after December 7, 1939? I figured that an abrupt departure around that time would have been suspicious. But really I would have settled for finding out his middle name. Or even just confirmation of his first.

The man told me that Foss had been sold in the 1980s, and

when it was sold, they destroyed the records predating the 1950s. He could look for someone by that name after 1950, but not before. I thanked him and hung up, feeling deflated.

I considered the idea that I might find a mention of Anderson in the local newspapers in connection with the *C.S. Holmes*. Had there been some terrible shipwreck? I used a historical newspaper aggregator to search for his name and any mention of the *C.S. Holmes*. I found articles about the *C.S. Holmes* but no mention of Anderson. And no shipwreck.

I moved on to the Social Security Death Index, looking online state by state. The Social Security Administration was founded in 1936, and though Anderson might not have been enrolled right away, eventually he would have been. Then, when he died, his social security number would have been made public, as would his death date and last known address. I looked at the records for every Ed Anderson, E. Anderson, and Anderson, born between 1903 and 1905, who died in Washington State. There were hundreds—but I couldn't confirm any were him. I combed through the California records with the same criteria, remembering Barbara's second runaway incident. Then I began looking at the whole West Coast. It was possible he had begun working for a new shipping company and settled there. I also looked at Maine, Massachusetts, Hawaii, and Alaska. Then I began the slog of looking through the whole country. There were thousands of E. Andersons. I isolated five men who I thought could be him and contacted a private investigator I knew, Conor McCourt, a former New York Police Department detective, who had offered to run the social security numbers through a system that might be able to give more information. There was an Edward J. Anderson who died in Chelan, Washington, when he was seventy-seven, but the report pulled up no possible relatives, no properties owned, no work history, or any of the other things it had promised. This was true for all the Andersons I had searched. They were a mass of indistinguishable Andersons.

I started to go through census records. The last year of publicly available census records is 1940, and it is the year after Barbara disappeared. I started my search with Seattle and expanded outward, eventually extending it to the entire country. I was able to rule out other Andersons either by their jobs or because they had children who were more than five years old, thinking that Anderson would have most likely mentioned a child in his last letter to Barbara. All Anderson bricklayers, lawyers, mechanics, and accountants were possibly him, but unlikely to be. All naturalized citizens were thrown out. All Andersons with eleven-year-old daughters were thrown out. I spent hours staring at my computer until my contacts dried on my eyes. I would sit down to search in the morning and look up from my screen to discover it was night. After months, I finished going through the census records. I hadn't found one person who definitively matched his description. I had no trace of him after 1935. I didn't know where else to look. It seemed that Anderson had disappeared, at least from paper records, around the same time as Barbara did.

Kickboxing and searching for Barbara and Anderson became my two most time-consuming endeavors. These pursuits provided a façade of order in an otherwise chaotic period in my life.

P.J. and I talked endlessly about our situation. We talked

about our uncertainty: Would we always feel this way? Would we stay together? But leaving felt unimaginable; I did not quite believe myself when I wondered this aloud. What, really, had happened? There was one point of contention that we couldn't seem to reconcile. There had been a disparity in our experiences. P.J. had spent a lot less time with Kristin than I had with Michael. Before the experiment began, we had discussed the importance of avoiding a tit-for-tat scenario. It would be punitive and petty, we agreed. But something wasn't sitting right with P.J. He was sheepish about comparing our experiences but couldn't seem to help himself.

"How is this not tit for tat?" I would ask him.

"I'm not saying that it's not. But it's also lots of other things."

In my mind, he was trying to quantify the unquantifiable. He wanted to determine if he had been taken advantage of or treated unfairly. In an open relationship there are certain societal taboos that the couple must confront, and these are different for men and women. For men, there is the fear of being cuckolded. You let your wife sleep with someone *else*? What kind of a *man* does that? For women, it's that they are reluctant polyamorists who are just trying to please the men they couldn't satisfy. I dismissed that idea as infantilizing—it depended on an outdated understanding of women's sexual complexity. But P.J. was having a harder time shaking the notion that his masculinity had been compromised. Had I betrayed him? And if so, how? We had technically agreed to all of it. This kind of betrayal felt unquantifiable. So P.J. turned to the things he could measure—days spent apart, words spoken or not spoken—and tried to tabulate them.

We were at an impasse. It occurred to me that there was a way around the parity question, at least. When we had first returned from Canada, Kristin had been out of town, and P.J. and she had plans to meet for a drink when she got back. I told P.J. that they could do whatever they wanted that night. I was tired of feeling like he was owed something. I was tired of feeling guilty. There was also a vindictiveness to what I was doing: maybe it was time for him to feel a little guilty too.

To make matters more guilt inducing, I was sick. It was nothing serious, a minor respiratory infection, a slightly glorified cold—but still, point for me.

"Are you sure about this?" P.J. asked, standing in the doorway of our bedroom, where I was reading and collecting a small mountain of snotty tissues. He looked uncertain, like an animal sniffing out food, wondering if it's a trap.

"Yes, please, go," I said, waving him away nonchalantly.

Once he was gone, I sat on my bed reading a book, blowing my nose, and hacking up phlegm. It occurred to me that I had created the exact scene that I had been so afraid of in the months before our experiment began. I was reading alone at night in a room while P.J. was out with another woman. The illness was an added cherry on top, making the scene more pathetic than I had imagined. Was it so awful? Not really. Mostly, there were too many things happening for me to be horrified by any one of them. And part of me was relieved. I felt on some level that I had emasculated P.J. I would remasculate him, then.

"We're still in the abyss," P.J. had said to me, rubbing my shoulder one night when I had gotten upset. "We don't know what to do, except to keep moving." We'll figure this out together, was what I took him to mean. But at home surrounded by my tissues, realizing that this scene was not as heartrending as I had imagined, made me feel like the oddest woman who had ever lived. I didn't care. I put my book away and called Michael.

Perhaps the most baffling part of being back in New York was that sometimes things proceeded normally, and this normalcy in the midst of a maelstrom only confused us more. P.J. and I still ate ice cream. We still had sex. We still huddled together on our tiny couch and watched movies. We babysat a friend's baby who slept in the stroller while we quietly ate beside him, terrified that he might wake up from his fierce, sweaty slumber and that we wouldn't know what to do with him. We walked a friend's dog. We both loved the dog and loved loving the dog together. We went grocery shopping and enjoyed plotting the things we would eat. We enjoyed the things we enjoyed no less during this time—perhaps even more.

And then there was Michael, whom I texted or spoke to on the phone every day. What were we to each other? A friend very reasonably asked me, "Aren't there ways to be close to people without sleeping with them?" Yes, of course. But the truth was that Michael and P.J. were the closest people to me in the world. Sex is a fast track to intimacy and it felt as though my skin was stitched to both of them.

It was now fall. The sharp clear air and the chimney fires and the homey smells of sweet things baking had made me nostalgic for a time when things were simpler. I realized that one of the things I had lost was a story: the simple story of marriage, with clean lines and a sensible narrative arc. I always imagined this told in the form of a toast at a golden anniversary. In that story, our devotion was unshakable, always growing rather than wobbling or retreating. The hard times were ordinary—sleepless nights with a colicky baby, money and work worries—and our union never in question. The hard times weren't really all that hard. But everyone knows that marriage doesn't easily accommodate the narrative form. A jagged edge always exposes this elegant love story as a farce.

One evening I went out for drinks with two friends, both of whom worked at progressive magazines and generally were difficult to shock. But when I told them about our marital experiment, they were horrified. They sat across from me in the dimly lit booth with their mouths literally agape, like shocked cartoon characters. They seemed to take my decision personally, as though somehow my arrangement endangered us all. One was about to get married (the drinks had been to celebrate her engagement, admittedly an inappropriate time to make my announcement), and the other was eager to find a more serious relationship.

"Ben and I could never do that," the engaged one said.

"Why?" I asked, wondering why she had specifically said her fiance couldn't, which suggested that maybe *she* could.

"He's too loyal," she said.

The comment stung. Were we not loyal? I didn't like to think of myself or P.J. as being disloyal. *We are loyal,* I wanted to say. *We don't think of it that way at all.* But I couldn't say anything because I was so wounded by the comment and felt suddenly unsure.

When I ordered an unusual cocktail and offered them a taste, the other friend declined, joking, "We don't want what you've got." I recalled how I had felt the first time P.J. and I had discussed not being monogamous. I had felt so suddenly untethered. The urge to jam my fingers in my ears had been overwhelming.

I had felt pigeonholed by the story of marriage, but now that I had complicated my own marriage, I longed for that simpler narrative. Commercials featuring happy couples made my heart twinge. I could not walk into home stores because they evoked visions of domestic utopia that were painful to me. Watching happy couples dining in restaurants, I was torn between thinking that they were desperately engaging in an elaborate charade and that I wanted to be one of them again. Did any part of that story still belong to me? Talking with friends in the midst of relationship problems, I had an urge to qualify everything I said with, "I know I've made some weird relationship decisions, but . . ."

One night P.J. and I went to an Italian restaurant not far from our house. The spaghetti was overcooked and P.J. was jittery. Michael would be visiting that weekend. Did he want to see Kristin again that weekend? Something about spending another night with her again so soon didn't seem like a good idea to him.

"Of course, I just want you all to myself," he said in passing. He was stuck, he said. He couldn't get over his visceral resistance to another man sleeping with me. But since he knew I wanted to—and of course he still wanted other women—there was no alternative but pressing on. Or stopping. Neither was right.

"Do you think you ever will be comfortable with the idea of my being with another man?" I asked.

He thought this over. "Not really. I think it will always feel like a punch in the gut. Maybe I'll learn to live with it, maybe I'll be able to twist it into something else. But I think I'll always be pierced by it."

I was struck with clarity. He was trying to intellectualize an animal instinct. And I could imagine him doing this forever: twisting, explaining, reexplaining, and still feeling stabbed. He was too proud to ask me to stop. It occurred to me then that this was the true pact of our marriage: it was a promise that neither of us would have to ask to be protected.

"It's over," I said. "I just want to be with you." I wasn't sure I meant it. I was saying the words to see if they felt true. And I wanted to save P.J., from me and from himself. His indecisive nature was overriding his instincts for self-preservation.

My initial feeling was disappointment. Then relief. It felt like I had just been pulled off a racetrack. I settled back into my chair. We talked more. We decided we would put things on hold. "It's a pause," I said. "Not a definite stop," P.J. said. We were deciding not to decide. One day, we hoped, the way forward would become more obvious. But as we talked, I wondered if we had flipped a switch that could not be flipped back.

The hard part was telling Michael he couldn't visit. I called him the next day, as I paced around the little park near my apartment. He was gracious, but hurt. "When you write about this," he said, "make me tall, charming, and handsome. Point out how tall I am—that I'm taller than P.J.," he said.

"You *are* taller than P.J.," I said.

"But really make the point."

And then, sounding wounded, he said, "You know, you didn't really do the experiment. The experiment was about freedom, about opening yourself to possibility, but in your mind, you always wanted to wind up in the same place. You never really considered starting a new life."

I didn't know what to say, but I thought that he might be right. "In a way, it's more beautiful like this," he said quickly. "I always thought your story and Barbara's story were running in parallel. But now I see that that's not true. Barbara's story is about running away and your story is about coming home."

NINETEEN

As I searched for Anderson, I continued to look directly for Barbara. I requested the police files from Boston and asked the Brookline police if they had any additional ones beyond what I had seen during my visit. The logbook, I was told, was all that remained. Because it had happened so long ago, the other files had been destroyed.

In 1952, Helen had contacted the Social Security Administration to find out if Barbara had had any earnings since her disappearance. When Barbara ran away at sixteen, Helen had been quite sure that she was capable of quickly finding work, and no doubt she would only have been more capable at twenty-five. But the Social Security Administration told her that this information was confidential. "Even if the regulations of the Administration permitted the disclosure of confidential information and we told you that we had no records of your daughter during the time she has been missing, such information would not be conclusive as to death. It is possible that she may have been unemployed or engaged in employment not covered by the Social Security Act." *Even if we told you that we had no records . . .* It wasn't a form letter, but something personally written by an administration employee addressing each of Helen's specific points. Had he looked? Had curiosity been too much and had he thought, *I'll just have a peek at the files,* and was this his veiled way of telling Helen there were no records? It seemed a stretch.

Helen had been wise to check with the Social Security Administration, even if she didn't have the legal right. Not having earnings would not have meant that Barbara was dead, but having them would have conclusively proven she was alive. And if Barbara had lived a regular life span anywhere in the United States, it was hard to imagine that she would never have worked again, though she could have gotten a fake social security card. She had always worked—from the time she was nine, and arguably even before that. Perhaps realizing that no great investigation was under way ten, fifteen, or even thirty years later she might have felt it was fairly innocuous to take a job for which she had to fill out tax and social security information, and considered it not worth falsifying those documents.

First, I checked the Social Security Death Index to ensure that no one with her name was in the system. There were no Barbara Newhall Folletts, and no Barbara Folletts who matched her description. There was a Barbara L. Follett, but the birth year didn't match. There were many Barbara Rogerses but I doubted she would have kept her married name for long, and there were too many to track each one. I created a file to pursue them as a last resort. There was also the possibility that she had changed her name to something else entirely. When she ran away to California, she had traveled under a pseudonym: K. Andrews. What I really needed was her social security number—which she would have been less likely to change than her name—to see if that number was tied to the Death Index. I decided to call her last employer in Brookline, on the off chance that they would, very unprofessionally, give me the number or any other information.

No such luck—they didn't keep records for that long. The woman on the phone suggested I could try their national offices, but she doubted they would have anything. I was keeping an ever-growing to-do list. At the top I listed more promising leads and at the bottom less promising ones. I put this toward the bottom.

I called the Social Security Administration. After a long wait, a man came on the line and I explained Barbara's story. She had been missing for over seventy-five years. Was there any way I could find out if someone with her social security number had been declared dead? Or had ever paid social security taxes after a certain date? The man on the other end of the line was baffled. "No one has ever asked me a question like that," he said, clearly delighted. "It's usually just wives calling to say their husbands are dead."

I could hear him typing on his computer, looking things up. He gave me the names of some forms I might have to fill out, either the 711 or the 714, and suggested I go to the Social Security Administration in person and discuss the matter with them. And then he paused. "Why do you want to know? Are you some kind of journalist?" I told him yes. "Oh, good," he said. And then he proceeded to tell me a long story about a girl he had known as a child in Cleveland who had gone missing. Her name was Beverly Potts.* He made me write her name down and confirm the spelling. "Maybe after you find this woman, you can look for her," he said.

There was a Social Security Administration office a few blocks down from my apartment and the next day I walked over. I took

*Beverly Potts's disappearance is considered one of Cleveland's most famous cold cases. In 1951, the ten-year-old went to a park with a friend. The friend left early and Potts was never seen again.

the elevator up to the sixth floor and entered a fluorescently lit room with rows of black plastic chairs. The waiting area was half full and everyone was bored and fiddling with their phones. I was quite possibly the only person in the history of people going to the Social Security Administration who was thrilled to be there. A man instructed me to take a number and wait in one of the chairs. The woman down the row from me was taking selfies, making a sexy pouty face. Another woman, speaking to an agent at the window behind me, seemed to be telling the agent her entire life story, including a long list of people she was no longer speaking to. There were birthday balloons in one of the offices. Occasionally the light chatter was broken by the piercing announcement over the intercom of the next number. After about half an hour, my number was called.

I explained to the agent why I was there. She looked at me bug-eyed and then thought for a long time. "Hold on one second," she said before getting up and returning with another woman, to whom I repeated the whole story. This woman looked at me bug-eyed too but was more assertive. "Are you related to this woman?" she asked. "No," I admitted. She shook her head, "A family member can file a claim, but you can't."

"But isn't there an age at which it's safe to presume that someone is dead?" I asked. "She would be a hundred and one if she were alive and she's been missing for seventy-five years," I said. "Yeah, she's probably dead," the woman said, but she shook her head again firmly. I wasn't family. And it was the administration's policy not to presume someone was dead until they were more than a hundred and twenty years old. I would just have to wait nineteen years.

I decided to try a different tactic. Barbara's family and friends had all believed that Barbara had run away, though the details of their theories differed. But if there was one obsession that gripped Barbara throughout her life, it was the sea. As her mother wrote in *Magic Portholes,* the other book she had written about their Caribbean and South Seas voyage, Barbara had a "sea madness—it's in her blood." She believed that the sea was her destiny, once pointing out to her mother that she was born a Pisces, "the water sign." And she was impulsive. She got an idea in her head and acted, logistics be damned. "Ask Barbara to wait?" her mother had scoffed during one of her bouts of sea obsession. "Might as well ask a Northern river to change its course." Barbara had described herself as being "haunted" by the sea. The sea had a voice, she said—it called to her. Helen wrote that the sea had a "mystery that was compelling her to go back to it."

I began going through ship manifests online, looking specifically for ships sailing to and from places Barbara had already been. St. Lucia had "felt like home." There was Barbados, Montserrat, Tahiti, the Tonga Islands, and Samoa. I looked at ships leaving from Seattle, thinking that she might have paid Anderson a visit, but I also looked at California, Boston, and New York, considering her familiarity with those places. I looked at Alaska as well, since Anderson might have been there. I searched using her married name and her maiden name.

It was a more conservative time. How many twenty-five-year-old women could have been traveling by ship alone in those days? Many, it turned out. I spent hours at the library scrolling through the names. I tried various iterations of her pseudonyms and spellings of her last names. I tried looking just for the name Barbara with her birth year. There were thousands of Barbaras traveling who were my Barbara's age. Barbara Rogerses abounded.

One night, after a particularly long day in the library scanning through ship manifests, I got home and had a sudden itch to check a few more before going to a kickboxing class. This happened often. Just one more search and I'll find her. I had become convinced that the information was out there somewhere. People left trails. Not as many as they do now, but when they traveled, their passports were stamped. When something noteworthy happened, there were newspaper stories. When they died, there were death certificates. I was nagged by the idea that the information must be available. If I just looked hard enough, or thought creatively enough, I would find it.

Sometimes a different variation of search terms would occur to me and I would have to check the manifests immediately. What if I tweaked the age range just a few more years? The manifests were handwritten. What if the person recording the information had gotten it wrong, or written illegibly? What if "26" accidentally became "28"? What if I listed Barbara's married name in the search terms but named her parents as relatives? The smallest changes in the search variables could turn up entirely different results.

Lying on my bed, trying these various search terms, a new manifest popped up for a Barbara Rogers. In March of the year that Barbara had disappeared, a twenty-five-year-old Barbara Rogers traveled from San Francisco to Hawaii. I froze. It was her. She had traveled to Hawaii before. I shouted for P.J. to come into the room.

"I found her," I said, dumbfounded.

"Are you sure?" P.J. asked.

"Yes!" I put my hands on my head. This was the biggest break yet, the only real break in what had felt at times like an impossible search. Finding the manifest revealed to me what I had always suspected and wanted to believe: she was out there. She had lived past December 7, 1939. She had run away. She had crossed the continent, gotten on a boat, and left. It was all so clear now. She had seized control of her life rather than letting other people determine it for her. She had triumphed. I had triumphed. I rapidly took screenshots of the manifest, irrationally concerned that the proof would somehow disappear. I saved the manifest on my computer and e-mailed it to myself.

"What are you going to do now?" P.J. asked.

"I don't know," I said. "I guess try to trace her steps after Hawaii?" I doubted she had stayed in Honolulu and suspected she had used it as a port of embarkation to other places, which was what she had done the last time she was there. It occurred to me to start looking right then, maybe stay up late into the night now that I had another clue. Maybe I would need to travel to Hawaii. That sounded nice. I took some notes. I could feel how frazzled I was. "I'm going to go to kickboxing to calm down a little. Meet me after and let's go to dinner. We'll go out." I was in a celebratory mood.

I jogged to my kickboxing class, which was a few neighborhoods away. I didn't mind the putrid smell as I ran over the oil-streaked Gowanus Canal because I was so amped up. I wasn't concerned about the dark, didn't bother switching to the other side of the road as I normally did when I passed the creepy abandoned parking lot. I was flying and felt invincible. Outside the kickboxing gym, I texted Michael. I e-mailed my grad school professor and my editor. Of course she had gone to sea, I thought again and went into the gym.

Class was especially packed that night with sweaty women

punching bags. I rolled my bag out to the middle of the floor and punched and kicked with more vigor than usual. I was midpunch when a thought occurred to me. Why had the manifest listed Barbara as twenty-five? In March, Barbara would have been twenty-six, unless the ship had sailed in the first four days of the month—her birthday was March 4. Not a big deal, I told myself. I would check the manifest when I got home. It could just be a mistake, a miscalculation on the part of the record keeper even if it was in the later part of the month. I kept punching. Then my stomach dropped. The manifest was stamped 1939. March 1939. A full nine months *before* Barbara had vanished. At that point, she would still have been living with her husband, oblivious to the affair and the threat of divorce. March 1940 would have been the right timing, not 1939.

How could I have made such a stupid mistake? I kicked the bag hard. I had been preoccupied since getting back from Canada, and sleep deprivation was making me frenzied and careless. I walked out of the gym into the cold, fall darkness utterly deflated. How had another Barbara Rogers traveled the same route Barbara had traveled before, just a year off? It seemed a cruel coincidence, a shadow Barbara taunting me. She was Eepersip darting through the forest; just when I thought I had gotten a hand on her wrist, she had wriggled from my grasp. I reminded myself that in a world of billions of people doing billions of things, cruel coincidences abound.

I texted Michael. I e-mailed my professor and my editor. "Never mind," I wrote. I walked to the bar to meet P.J., told him about my mistake, and quickly ordered a beer, slumping in my seat. I ordered the least healthy thing on the menu. Health suddenly seemed pointless. P.J. and I had planned to walk the two miles home after the meal, but as we stood outside in the dark, it began to rain lightly and I suggested we take a cab. We never took cabs. But I couldn't muster up the energy to wait on the subway platform. I just wanted to curl up in bed, possibly forever.

In the taxi, I watched the rain-blurred storefronts go by. I had felt so close to finding her, and now she seemed impossibly beyond my grasp. I had believed that it was just a matter of looking, of trying hard enough. But suddenly, finding a single person among the billions of people who have lived and are living on this planet seemed absurd. Perhaps it was naive to believe that people leave marks on the world, that we are not churned back into the earth like dead leaves in a compost pile. I had heard once that in a hundred million years, all buildings will be gone. Paper will exist, but the ink will vanish, so everything will be blank. Eternal blankness —forever. Why resist if that is our fate? I didn't even know my own great-grandparents' names. They had lived entire complex lives, had careers, had created homes and raised children. They had wanted things. Their children had known about them, their grandchildren less so but still some, and I knew nothing. As of 1990 between sixty thousand and a hundred thousand people were missing in the United States. I recalled the Brookline police logbook. Even that had a lot of missing people in it—a husband who didn't come home for dinner, then turned up later at the local pub, the twenty-two-year-old girl who slit her wrists and then walked out of her house.

A year after Barbara disappeared, Wilson wrote, "This is someone of striking presence, of glowing beauty, impossible not to notice in a room, a street, a subway, a crowd; a person twenty-five years old, born into an excellent family, five years married into another, and surcharged with distinction, with talents, as no one using half an eye could help perceiving in her carriage, the free swing of her stride, the quiet inner power she radiates unaware; an important being, one in ten million, and—don't you see?—*my daughter!*"

I had presumed, like Wilson, that our physical hold on the world was stronger, that we couldn't slip so easily into the unseen masses, especially if you were someone like Barbara, so brilliant, so lively, and for a brief flicker of time, so noticed. But those things didn't seem to matter. No one was exceptional; nothing lasted.

TWENTY

I woke up the next morning feeling galvanized rather than discouraged. Almost finding Barbara had given me a taste of what
it would feel like to really find her. I had told myself that the
mysterious ending was more elegant. Like Eepersip, Barbara was
the ephemeral wood nymph. I had believed that the mundane
facts would dilute the fantasy. Finding out that she had lived
most of her life in a quiet neighborhood in Colorado and raised
three sons would have been disappointing. Even if she had done
something more unconventional, becoming one of the few female
ship captains, it still wouldn't live up to my expectations. The
idea that she could be anywhere, could have done anything,
was seductive. Her many possible lives tantalized more than any
one life ever could. But sitting on my bed, taking screenshots
of the ship manifest, I had been given a touch of what it would
feel like to know.

I began going through the grave index, an online database where
you can search graves by name and state. At Cypress Lawn Me-
morial Park in San Mateo, California, I found a Barbara Follett
who was buried in 1992. She had the same birthday as Barbara,
March 4, but a different year. This Barbara, Barbara *Lee* Follett,

was three years older than my Barbara, and she constantly popped up in my searches, making my heart skip a beat.

I spent most of my time searching through travel records. I recalled that once Anderson had asked Barbara if she was writing under the pseudonym Barbara Hardy. He had recently seen an article for a seasickness cure by a Barbara Hardy and wondered if it was hers. Yes, I could see Barbara Follett becoming Barbara Hardy. It sounded like the kind of name she might pick. I searched it. A twenty-five-year-old Barbara Hardie had traveled to Hawaii in 1939. My heart jumped. But my previous experience had made me steelier, more clinical. I opened the manifest. It was for June 1939—before Barbara disappeared.

In 1947, eight years after Barbara vanished, a Barbara Rogers took a Pan Am flight from Bermuda to New York. Had she gone to Bermuda only to return later? This Barbara Rogers was traveling with someone: Edward Rogers. The name struck me. A strange coincidence. I scrolled over to the next column that listed the ages. They didn't match.

A Katherine Newhall who was Barbara's age traveled from San Francisco to Honolulu in 1943. Her profession: librarian. Barbara had used K in a pseudonym before. I added her information to the file. A Barbara Newell hiked across the U.S. border into Canada in 1954. I saved her information too. But later I was able to rule them both out.

When I found a Barbara Rogers traveling from Havana, Cuba, to Miami in 1940, it gave me pause. I opened the manifest and read and stopped suddenly when I noticed another name: Elwood E. Anderson. He was thirty-four years old, roughly the age Anderson should have been at that time. I scrolled down to Barbara's age. Twenty-three. Not the right age. I was about to click out of the document when I noticed a small mark next to the "23." It was a very faint 6, as if the typewriter key had landed on the paper but without quite enough ink. A ghost 6. Had the person recording her age meant to write "26"? *That* would have been the right age. I downloaded and saved the manifest, so I could look into it further.

One afternoon in the library, I used Stanford's copyright renewal database to look up *The House Without Windows*. A renewal record came up for the novel. I clicked on it. It had been renewed on December 10, 1954, almost fifteen years to the day after Barbara vanished. I scrolled down. "Renewing entity: Mrs. Nickerson Rogers (Barbara Newhall Follett)." I jumped out of my seat, my heart pounding, feeling like I had seen a ghost.

I took screenshots of the renewal notice. I imagined a middle-aged Barbara on a chaise longue on a beach, lackadaisically filling out a renewal form that she would later drop in the mail from whatever exotic location she was in. She had cut all ties with her former life, but she harbored a protective fondness for that first book, the one she wrote when she still lived with her father, when she was making up her own language and dreaming of the wild life.

I contacted the publisher but couldn't get through to anyone on the phone, so I sent an e-mail and heard nothing. I contacted my publisher and asked about their copyright renewal policy, assuming that publishing houses used the same standards. I was told that renewals were handled by the publisher, not by the author, but were done in the author's name. It was unlikely that Barbara had had anything to do with it.

The next day, I had a phone call with Paul Collins, the journalist and literary investigator at Portland State University who had written the magazine piece in which I first learned about Barbara. I was eager to talk to him because, though his article mentioned Barbara's disappearance, it didn't make reference to a search for her. I wanted to know if he had tried to find her.

He was friendly and generous on the phone, touched that something he had written had resulted in such large interest. He had not looked for her, he said. I quickly mentioned the copyright renewal notice and he said he had come across the same thing and had been similarly stunned. But he agreed with my publisher. At the time of his research, he had requested the copyright renewal paperwork from the Library of Congress and had come to the conclusion that Knopf had probably done it in her name. He e-mailed me the file. It was a simple typewritten form listing unremarkable details about the book. The address given was Knopf's. There was no signature.

Looking for Barbara reminded me of a ghost story a friend had once told me. Her grandfather had died and one day not long after, her grandmother was walking through the house when she heard the sharp crack of her husband's cough in the hall nearby. She froze. How could this be? It had so plainly, so unmistakably been the cough she had heard for so many years. I considered it a grief-stricken hallucination driven by the expectation of hearing her husband cough again. The mishearing of a branch scratching against a window was the mind's refusal to understand that what is gone is gone. The more I looked, the more I saw these almost-Barbaras, these mirages everywhere.

One day, I was flipping through the end of *Lost Island* again and it struck me differently:

Sometime, not too far off, she would stage another rebellion. It would not be the same kind of rebellion, though. One could never repeat the real adventures. That was why so many people were unhappy, she reflected. They tried to go back and repeat all the things that had made them happy before. They tried to retrace the trail and visit again the places where they had known their highest ecstasies; whereas, if only they had the courage to push on, forward, over deserts and swamps and glaciers, they would sometime make new discoveries as bright as the others, or even brighter, perhaps. . . .

If we assume that Barbara continued to subscribe to that philosophy, I had been looking in all the wrong places. The fact that she had been to Honolulu before didn't matter. She wouldn't retrace her steps. She would break out into an entirely new adventure——an entirely new life. The whole world was an option.

TWENTY-ONE

Fall marked the beginning of my shadow life. Something small but elemental had changed in the texture of my marriage. Like a pattern in a knit rug in which the needle had slipped, a seemingly minor error had sent the whole design askew. Indefinitely pausing the marital experiment loosened something in my fantasy life, allowing me to imagine in richer detail what my life with Michael would have been like. I was protected by the conviction that I had made my decision, I had picked P.J., so a little fantasizing seemed harmless. One evening I was setting the table—P.J. and I had just run around the corner to grab Indian takeout, and then we were going to watch a movie—and as I set a plate down, I realized I was happy. And then a memory of Michael occurred to me.

"In our life," Michael had told me, "you would be sitting at the table writing. You would be fretting about something structural in the draft, and I would reassure you. I would be standing in the kitchen making red sauce for pasta, stirring the onions." The vividness of the details, how clearly he saw our life together, had touched me. But at the time, I had dismissed it. In his fantasy, I had thought, we are always in *his* house, doing something domestic. In his fantasy, he was just inserting me into his life. And he was telling me a story whose ending I already knew: a lovely, quiet life, a long marriage, children, houses. That wouldn't sustain me, I had thought. But now, pulling the Indian food out of the brown bags and setting it on my own table, I saw the scene at Michael's table clearly and it gripped me. Maybe it *was* what I wanted. Or maybe it was what I wanted *sometimes*.

There were two lives now: the one I was living and the one I was not, and they were stitched together awkwardly, helplessly dragging each other around. Something I did in my real life would provoke a fantasy of my unlived life. I would open a can in my kitchen, and suddenly I would imagine opening a can in Michael's kitchen. P.J. would cough in the other room, and suddenly I would think, what if it were Michael coughing in the other room? If I felt happy, if I felt anything, my shadow life tagged along, forcing me to imagine the correlated moment in the life I was not living.

Previously, if I had regretted anything it was that I got to live only one life. I remember thinking as a kid how sad it was that I couldn't be a veterinarian, a journalist, *and* the first woman in the NBA. How disappointing to have to choose. How disappointing that I couldn't live in the jungle and the mountains and the city. But now that I was living two lives, it wore me out. I saw how a double life, the alluring possibility of the other life, could haunt and poison all my joy.

I tried to will the shadow life away. *This is lovely,* I would remind myself as P.J. and I walked through the park. *I don't want anything else.* It *was* lovely. But something remained blocked in my interactions with P.J. I had never imagined that two people who talked as much as we did would ever have trouble communicating. But I was beginning to understand that it was not the amount of words but the kinds of words that needed to be said, and we were both groping for them. It felt as though we were standing before an enormous closed door, guessing at the password and being refused entry.

There was something wolflike and wary in our interactions. We never shouted. We were considerate of each other, cooking for each other, doing the little household chores that the other one did not like. P.J. made the bed. I swept. We circled each other, waiting for the other to make the first move. I wanted him to make some heartfelt declaration that he wanted me. "I love you, you're my best friend. And no matter what, I'm always going to take care of you," he said one day as we were talking after dinner and I had gotten upset. Previously, a comment like this would have annoyed me. It implied that I couldn't take care of myself and besides, it was independence I craved, not coddling. But now, overwhelmed by independence, I found the idea of being taken care of comforting. But what he was describing seemed sad—seemed to imply that he would take care of me, despite some separation between us. I imagined living in separate houses, his coming over to shovel my driveway after a snowstorm or to drop off some groceries. I would be standing in the window, giving him a sad little wave. He would be standing outside, returning my sad little wave. Then he would leave. "It feels like I've been stabbed in the gut," he said at one point. "I think we stabbed each other. I think we stabbed ourselves."

In comparison, the untrodden life shimmered with possibility. "Don't forget," Michael had said. "Either way, you're giving up a marriage. One just hasn't happened yet."

When I planned a trip to see some college friends and P.J. couldn't come because of work, I had the sense that he was relieved that we would be apart. I compared him to Michael, who seemed to want nothing more than to be around me. Sitting on his couch watching television would have been a momentous event. Dinner would have been a momentous event. He became frantic when I was slow to text back, and when I woke up in the morning I would have texts from the middle of the night telling me that he was sad I wasn't with him. The comparison was unfair. Of course the man I had been with for years, the man with whom I was struggling to communicate, would be less thrilled to see me. I knew it was unfair, but those kinds of comparisons became irresistible.

I spoke to friends about my predicament. "You're going to have to cut off connections with this other guy if you want to save your marriage," they counseled me wisely. But it was very hard for me to see Michael as some *other guy*, faceless, without his own pains and needs. And cut off connection with the only person who seemed to understand me anymore, just as the person who I relied on for unconditional regard seemed indifferent to my presence? Then I would truly be alone, I thought.

I'm not sure exactly when I began toying with the idea of leaving, but I know the idea struck me with full force one day during a run in Prospect Park. As I rounded the bend for a second lap, an idea occurred to me. What if P.J. and I separated until Christmas? I could go back to Myanmar, report a story I had been mulling over, while P.J. continued his work in New York. I was feeling overwhelmed by the needs of two men and thought some time alone focusing on something other than myself might be just what I needed. Working alone would fortify me with some of that solitary strength I had felt over the summer. It would give us both space to reflect on whether we wanted to continue our marriage. I had a sense that cycling between indifference and pleasantness in New York was not going to help anything. Did one or both of us need to make some grand, sweeping gesture? I considered the idea that we needed to banish ambivalence from our lives, but wasn't sure how to do that. P.J. and I had plans to go out for drinks at a wine bar that night. I would discuss it with him then.

During this period, Wilson Follett was often on my mind. I had been so quick to judge him, but now I found myself considering more compassionate interpretations of his decisions. I wondered if Wilson's behavior could be explained by a desire to avoid a shadow life. Rather than wondering what that new life with a new family in a different place had to offer, he went and found out. Like him, I was feeling the pull of someone outside my marriage. I saw myself not as unfaithful or fickle, but as a person with complicated desires in a complicated situation who was trying simultaneously to do what was right for others and best for myself.

When a marriage falls apart, it is tempting, especially when affairs are involved, to see the adulterer as the villain and the wronged spouse as the victim. From the outsider's perspective, the adulterer is marked. *Once a cheater, always a cheater,* as the saying goes. *He is the type of person who cheats,* people say, as if there were something corrupt at the person's core. A married male friend of mine had once gotten drunk and made out with a girl at a bar. It struck me as a relatively harmless mistake, but I was surprised when his wife told me. It did seem out of character. I couldn't really picture this particular guy going out to a bar, getting drunk, and making out with a random person. He cooks elaborate, healthy dinners with his wife every night, portioning just the right amount for leftovers so that he can bring them to work in Tupperware containers. He undertakes labor-intensive home improvement schemes. He actually has a five-year plan. The couple had gone to therapy, but the one who seemed to be struggling the most with the drunken error in judgment was the husband. His wife told me, "I have to keep reminding him that though this happened he's still a good man." He felt tainted.

I once read an article about "a cheating gene," which suggested that certain humans are "biologically inclined to wander."[*] The author marvels that this phenomenon applies to women too, which struck me as old-fashioned. But despite this apparently biological impetus, 91 percent of Americans find it morally wrong. Cheaters with their cheating natures are forever trapped inside their villainy. Of course, my situation was different than your run-of-the-mill adultery. But as I continued to have contact with Michael, and on some level allow myself to live in and even enjoy my shadow life, I felt marked.

During Wilson's affair with Margaret, he had existed in the murky space between one relationship in which he felt remade and one in which he felt undone. At the very least, I found it admirable that he hadn't drawn the affair out, hadn't subjected either woman to the ego-withering humiliation of entering into a contest for his affection. He had sought clarity, had refused to live in the shadow space between two loves, and then he had embraced his decision, discarding all that came before. Maybe it was cruel not to give Helen more of a chance. But I began to

---

[*] Richard A. Friedman, "Infidelity Lurks in Your Genes," *New York Times,* May 22, 2015.

wonder if perhaps it was not crueler to hold someone in limbo while you decide his or her fate. And what if staying were cruel? There is something unkind about staying when you don't want to, letting your spouse know that though all feeling has been drained from your marriage you dutifully remained anyway. Every Christmas Eve, every Sunday picnic, every happy moment would have the potential to be poisoned by the lover wondering whether he or she was not your lover, but your captor.

One afternoon not long after I got back from Canada, I pulled out the file that I kept on Wilson. I spent the day going through his book, his letters, and the letters his family had written about him. I wanted to see what happens when you leave.

Wilson and Margaret had three children, two sons and a daughter. Their daughter, Jane, who was five when Barbara vanished, would later write, "I almost never heard him talk about his past (even the portion of his past that was within my memory)." And "His worst flaw was his willingness to walk away from uncomfortable situations."

In 1947, he abandoned them. Jane was twelve and she wrote him a letter begging him to come home: "We are underclothed. We do not have a good school. Our father is not with us." They were eating bread, tomatoes, a little meat, but they didn't have enough food. The boys were taking their anger out on Margaret, who was on the verge of a nervous breakdown. She told Jane that she was losing her mind, which must have terrified the twelve-year-old. "Growing children and a mother need their father," Jane wrote. "They can live without him, but something important is missing . . . It would be different if their father were dead." She ended her letter simply, "Come."

Jane's letter so exactly recalled the one Barbara had written when Wilson left. The two half sisters were roughly the same age when he abandoned them. Daughters morphed into new daughters begging him to come home, and his answer was always the same: no. This was the third time he had abandoned his children, but the first two times he had left, he had done so in order to enter into the exact same arrangement: family life, where there was never enough time for writing or the outdoors. After he left Margaret, he didn't start a new family. Perhaps he was too old (he was in his sixties). Or perhaps he had finally understood something about himself. Though he might have the capacity to love women and children, he was not a family man and could never be happy in a life like that for long. Family hadn't trapped Wilson. He had trapped himself.

By 1963, sixteen years after his abrupt departure, he was dying of emphysema. He was living in a spartan room in a boardinghouse in Kew Gardens in Queens. Jane was the only child he was on good terms with. He didn't have much of a relationship with his sons. He had never been close to Grace, Barbara was gone, and he hadn't seen Sabra since she was four. By now she would have been nearly forty. At the time of his divorce from Helen, Wilson claimed that Sabra was the one person who had made him reconsider leaving the family and that she "was always much more to me than you thought or than I had any way of expressing." But he never saw her again, not once, for the rest of his life. Sabra's second husband told me that when she was in college, she had tried to reach out to her father, but he had demurred. He believed that what he had done was for the best. In one of his many letters to Helen about their divorce, he wrote, "I realize that to vacillate for [Sabra's] sake, or for anyone's, would ultimately be the worse for her and me and everyone."

227

He wasn't entirely alone at the time of his death. He had friends in New York, and he still traveled to Vermont occasionally. He was immersed in his work, finishing his book on editing, *Modern American Usage,* and writing a critique of the most recent edition of *Webster's Ninth New Collegiate Dictionary* in the *Atlantic.* He was comfortably untethered from family life but not without connections. He was separated from Margaret, but still in touch. And though his relationships with his other children were strained, Jane and he corresponded about everything. He read the books she was reading in her college courses so they could write to each other about them. Perhaps love came more easily to Wilson in absentia.

At the time of his death, Wilson had almost no possessions and very little money. He hadn't been the literary success he had hoped to be. *No More Sea* was out of print. Jane marveled at how few papers he had left behind. He had always written letters quickly and didn't keep the responses. He didn't keep copies of his own published work, perhaps because it seemed vain and he was contemptuous of fame. It was another kind of vanishing, an erasure of himself from families, friends, letters, and work. And perhaps he was also erasing the people he had loved.

The sparseness of the end of his life, in terms of both people and possessions, made me wonder if he had ever envied Barbara's vanishing. She had managed something he could not—had just slipped out from underneath the things that burdened her. I thought again of the end of *The House Without Windows,* when Eepersip becomes "invisible for ever to all mortals, save those few who have minds to believe, eyes to see." It now read to me like a death scene.

In death, we are loved in absentia, but in a way that doesn't bind. We are liberated from others' expectations. We exist in mind only. Whoever had written that scene, whether it was Barbara or Wilson, had entertained a death fantasy. Death is the only truly clean escape. It is the departure for which we cannot be blamed, the place from which we cannot be tempted to return. There is no ambivalence in death. We are finally released from the things that dog us. And perhaps most important, we are released from ourselves. If death had been an escape for Eepersip, it had also been one for Wilson's characters. That was how he envisioned the end of the Teaswiths' tragic ancestral pattern: at the end of his book, everyone is dead. Death is the only way out. And it was the factor that I hadn't wanted to consider in Barbara's case.

That night P.J. and I sat in the window of a bar looking out on Atlantic Avenue. I told him about my separation idea. His eyes widened with worry. "Is that what you want?" he asked. I told him I didn't know, but that I just wanted something to change, and the uncertainty had become torturous. He asked what I meant and I explained the Myanmar plan. "But I want to go too," he said with a smile. I explained that I thought if we were separated, whatever was stuck would become unstuck, that if we really felt like we were losing each other, our indifference would evaporate. And if it didn't, then maybe we shouldn't be together.

We joked about this sort of bizarre fantasy where we were divorced, but still best friends, romantic best friends, we said. We would live in separate houses, perhaps around the corner from each other, perhaps we would even have children and dogs together, and when we were lonely, we would call one another on the telephone, and go out for dinner and talk for hours. As we talked, I stopped thinking of or even looking at the people passing by outside the bar's window. We recalled the feelings that had driven us to the arrangement in the first place: a sense that marriage was somehow insufficient. We wanted to be more than married, and now the talk of a separation seemed to be literally pulling us closer. We were leaning forward on our barstools, talking animatedly and laughing.

I told P.J. that if we were separated, there would be no reason to act cheerfully when I didn't feel cheerful, no reason for me to talk in a forced singsong voice that I hated but at times couldn't help but speak in now. I was trying a little too hard to be happy, to make him happy. I wanted to plaster over our problems with optimism. But it wasn't working. "We've always been closest when we're direct," P.J. said. "Even when it's sad or hard, even when you say something that pierces me. Right now, I feel close to you."

In separation, P.J. and I decided, we could just be what we were: two people who had no idea what they were doing, didn't really understand their own feelings, and were exhausted from trying. We would be free to feel as shitty as we wanted without the pressure of trying to fix it, or even name it.

When I was in elementary school, my best friend's parents got divorced. The mother had been so raw—and so fascinating to me. I was used to adults concealing unpleasantness from their children, but my friend's mother simply couldn't be bothered. She was all jagged edges, rage, tears, and occasionally laughter. Friends surrounded her. She was always off to lunch with someone to discuss her situation. She said the word "fuck" within earshot and once came back from dinner smelling like cigarettes. Sometimes at night when I slept over, I could hear her crying on the telephone. It was probably hellish for her, but I remember wanting to spend more time at their house during the divorce, not less.

I was of course romanticizing divorce and had no real concept of what it was like. But as P.J. and I joked about our imagined amicable divorce (that really sounded basically like a marriage) and continued to talk, I realized we were having fun. "My old friend," P.J. said, suddenly looking at me, stopping to marvel at what had happened. "Everything is going to be okay," he said. He told me he didn't want to separate, but he would if it was what I needed. Knowing that he didn't want to separate made me not want to separate. We walked home holding hands.

Four days later, I felt the coldness creep back again.

TWENTY-TWO

Finding Barbara—someone whose whereabouts had perhaps been deliberately concealed—seemed nearly impossible. But finding Anderson shouldn't have been. He was, in theory, a regular person, leaving the paper trail that regular people leave. So why couldn't I find him? Frustrated, I acknowledged the limits of my investigative capacities and sought help. I contacted an archivist at the Smithsonian, Marisa Bourgoin, who had a special penchant for finding unfindable, possibly long-dead people. We talked about doing the same for Barbara, but she agreed that Anderson should be easier to find, so we would start there.

One morning, I compiled everything I knew about Anderson—when he worked where, the names of the ships he had sailed on, the names of the captains of those ships, the few addresses I had—and sent it off to her and waited.

The next night, P.J. and I went out to dinner, and when I got home I happened to check my e-mail before going to sleep. The archivist had found Anderson. There were two attachments to her e-mail, both *Seattle Times* articles.

In May 1937, Edward A. Anderson got married. He hadn't told Barbara—he hadn't been in touch with her in two years. His wife, Wilma Crayne, was much younger, barely twenty-one to Anderson's thirty-three. The couple lived in Seattle, where

Anderson had been living the last time he wrote to Barbara. He continued to work for Foss, despite his insistence three years earlier that he had had enough, and would go on only two more tours, after which he would move to Alaska and live off the land.

From the very beginning, Anderson's marriage didn't go well. He was an enigma to his young wife. According to Wilma, "he seemed to have something on his mind," but when she asked him what that something was he grumbled, "You wouldn't understand."

On October 5, 1937, Anderson and Wilma got in a taxi to visit Wilma's mother in Toppenish, a tiny town located on an Indian reservation about 150 miles southeast of Seattle. The couple had a car, but Anderson told his wife he didn't feel like driving. When the taxi reached Yakima, a mere half hour from Wilma's mother's house, Anderson told her that he no longer wanted to go to his mother-in-law's, that she should go on without him. They went to a hotel in Yakima. Anderson told the taxi driver to wait while he took his wife inside. Inside the hotel room, he began acting strange.

"Well, you'll never hear from me again," he told Wilma, only moments later to contradict himself, saying, "I'll give you a ring tomorrow." He rummaged through his shaving kit. When he left, his wife noticed that he had taken his straight razor, leaving the safety razor, shaving cream, and brush.

Anderson got back into the cab and instructed the driver to take him back to Seattle. But about two hours into the trip, at Naches Pass, probably along the scenic U.S. Route 410, which runs through the Cascade Mountain range, he told the driver to stop, and he got out of the car.

"You go on alone," Anderson told him, "I'm going to walk

the rest of the way." Naches Pass is about eighty miles from Seattle. The driver protested, but Anderson wouldn't get back in the car, so he drove off, leaving him on a deserted stretch of highway in the mountains. Pine needles covered the ground. Alpine tundra surrounded him as he walked, with craggy rock faces sloping upward from the road and mountain peaks in the distance. The driver stopped and let Anderson catch up to him to check if he had changed his mind.

"No," Anderson told him. "You've been paid. Now get out of here and leave me alone." The cabby drove off, leaving Anderson by himself in the woods. Four days later, Wilma returned to Seattle and discovered that Anderson wasn't there. The driver had stopped by their address in Seattle and told Anderson's boss, who also lived there, what had happened in the cab. Wilma called the police. The next day, a search party with bloodhounds convened on Naches Pass. The cab driver and Anderson's boss came along—Anderson was supposed to have come to work the day before. They found nothing. Anderson had vanished.

One month later, a man's body washed up in the chilly autumn surf of Falmouth, Massachusetts, not far from Martha's Vineyard. The papers in the drowned man's pocket indicated that he owned a small boat, lived at 66 Ewing Street in Seattle, and was a native of Maine. There was also a banknote for a large withdrawal the man had made around the time of his marriage that May. He was identified as Edward Anderson. He had drowned in an apparent suicide. Barbara hadn't run off with him. He had been dead for two years by the time she vanished.

Anderson's death seemed to create more questions than it

provided answers. What was he doing on the other side of the country? It had been a month since he was last seen. What had he done in the meantime? Was there any significance to his being in Massachusetts, albeit eighty miles from Barbara? I now knew he was from Maine, though he had lived mostly in Seattle. Why had he been in Massachusetts at all? I was struck by the similarities of his and Barbara's stories, both of them walking out on their spouses and then disappearing a mere two years apart. One body was found. One was not. The sea had been essential to both of them. It seemed that Anderson, in an apparent state of despair, had gone back to the sea to die. The extreme alienation of the last months of his life—his dreams of Alaska thwarted, his own dramatic exit replete with its striking scenery—was unsettling. It made me rethink Barbara's story.

Had Barbara known about Anderson's death? It seemed highly unlikely. If she had known, she would have told their mutual friends. At the very least, she would have told her mother, who had been close to him, or Alice. But none of them knew.

While Anderson was missing, Barbara had been traveling to New Hampshire on the weekends, where she and Nick were renting a little farmhouse near Squam Lake. They were busily decorating, bringing old furniture from Nick's family's attic. Wilson had given them a kitchen range. They were repairing the floors, plastering parts of the walls, and building fires to keep warm while they worked. They hoped that when winter came, the little farmhouse could be a skiing headquarters.

It is possible that after her disappearance, Barbara went to Seattle, or to the last address she had for Anderson, and there she would have found out the truth. Or maybe she hadn't tried to contact him at all. Maybe she had never given him a second thought after that final letter. I had wanted to believe a different story, which now sounded cliché: girl is rejected by her husband, but says screw you, leaves him, and returns to her true love. But Anderson's death revealed that unless someone was lying, it appeared she had never spoken to a soul she had known from her previous life. It was a total severing that, while certainly possible, was hard to imagine.

TWENTY-THREE

Shortly before Thanksgiving, I went to Charlottesville for the weekend for my college roommate's thirtieth birthday. I drove two friends and their husbands. P.J. stayed home and worked. The whole weekend I felt solitary, aware of myself as distinct from the other couples, though not necessarily in a negative way. I observed them closely. Traveling reveals the inner workings of a relationship in a way that can be hard to otherwise observe. How they make plans, how they pack, and how they deal with money is telling. I found myself marveling at them in the way that a floundering swimmer might admire a graceful one.

My friend's birthday celebration was a surprise party thrown in a lavish resort by her significantly older boyfriend, whom none of us had met. The bartender wore a tuxedo. Filet mignon was on the menu. There were ornate flower arrangements. None of us really belonged in that formal environment and this became increasingly apparent as the night wore on. Much to the horror of the staff and the other, mostly middle-aged, plaid- and argyle-wearing clientele, we got very drunk—my best friend from college incredibly so. I recalled all the fights we had gotten into as a result of her drinking. I had never known how to deal with her when she was like that; all my attempts to convince her to stop drinking or calm down, or just leave, had been met with ire. But the years since college had distanced us. We hardly saw one another anymore. She got increasingly drunk and took off her dress to go skinny-dipping in the resort's outdoor infinity pool hot tub. She wasn't my problem anymore, I told myself. Her husband was there. He could deal with her. On her way back to the great chandeliered hall, she slipped and fell on a slate in the garden, badly bruising her thigh. She sat next to me on the leather couch, her hair sopping, speaking too loudly, exhorting me to touch her bruise, which was swelling and giving off heat. I waited for something mortifying to happen. I had visions of the immaculately dressed doormen grabbing us by our coats and tossing us into the night. But her husband appeared and, with total grace and patience, convinced her to lower her voice, to ice the enormous bruise, and to get in a cab and leave. I sat on the couch alone watching what was perhaps to most people a sordid scene of a marriage in the throes of substance abuse. But I saw something else. I saw a man who viewed his life as utterly tied to his wife's. Leaving wasn't an option. Yelling wasn't practical. He knew exactly what she needed to hear. He understood the minute fluctuations of her temperament. He would take care of her. As I watched him put her shoes on, drape her jacket over her shoulders, and help her through the enormous front door, I was suddenly aware of exactly what I had lost.

Michael once said of our relationship that I was a blue planet and he was a solitary space traveler passing by who had been pulled into my orbit and had suddenly found that he was home. "I'm still just passing the beautiful pale blue dot of another planet that I almost got to live on," he said to me when I broke it off.

I was touched by the analogy. But I didn't like my role as some bulky planet while he got to be the space cowboy. And now I thought of P.J. We were like two planets orbiting each other, too close and then too far. We had inched out of each other's orbit and then found ourselves alone in the dark. I have heard that this is what will happen to the universe. It won't gather in on itself and implode. It will disperse, its celestial bodies gradually drifting apart into the abyss. This gentle annihilation is somehow much more terrifying. I missed the pull of P.J.'s planet.

I recalled how, on a recent trip to Arkansas, my ninety-year-old grandfather had declared that he needed someone to trim his toenails. Normally, he went to a podiatrist to have them cut, but he said he was too tired to go out. Without hesitation P.J. offered to clip them. He pulled out a kitchen stool, laid down a bed of newspaper below my grandfather's feet, and gingerly worked away while my grandfather, a retired Navy captain who is quite comfortable giving orders, reclined in his La-Z-Boy instructing him. "That nail is hard to get," he said, telling P.J. to use the other clippers, which looked like pliers. It had been unpleasant. P.J. told me afterward that strange things happen to the feet of old men. But he had embraced the job and acted as though he handled old men's feet all the time. He hadn't let my grandfather feel ashamed. I remembered watching the scene, feeling bowled over by his kindness.

After Charlottesville, I went to my parents' house in D.C. P.J. was supposed to meet me a couple of days later so we could do Thanksgiving at his parents' house. My nerves were ragged. I wasn't sleeping and didn't have the energy to play the happy young couple. But now, after the trip, I felt stronger. Everything wasn't going to be horrible forever. I called him from my childhood bedroom.

"Can I be yours again?" I said. I didn't care about freedom anymore. I didn't care about whether it was possible to be bound but independent, loved but not possessed. I cared nothing for marriage in general, only for *my* marriage. The infinite possibilities of a life without attachment had left me and the people I loved floating in the infinite darkness of space. I could call it an anchor. I could call it a cage. But either way, I wanted it back.

"Yes," P.J. said. "I want to be yours again too."

TWENTY-FOUR

One morning before that Thanksgiving, I called Conor McCourt again, the former NYPD detective. I gave him a quick overview of Barbara's story: the childhood, the early publishing success, the runaway incidents as a teenager, the ship adventures, the marital problems. I was thinking that things were sounding pretty bad for Nick when I asked him, "Does anything immediately jump out at you?"

He paused. And then: "Suicide."

"What?" I said.

"Suicide," he repeated. Then the call dropped.

Barbara had seemed too buoyant for suicide. I took the end of *Lost Island* as an example of this. Even when Jane is forced to leave the island and return to New York, and Davidson leaves her, Barbara writes that Jane "will stage another rebellion"—but also that Jane was "saved for a more glamorous doom." I had brushed aside the doom part, chalking the language up to youthful melodrama. Barbara could be extravagant with her phrasing, sometimes preferring terms that were more colorful than precise. She described the father figure in *Lost Island* as having "dreams of luxurious senility." It sounds nice. I imagine an older gentleman lolling about on velvet chairs, savoring his senile fantasies, but I doubt that's what she meant. Similarly, maybe she liked the sound of a more glamorous doom but didn't quite mean it. Or did she?

McCourt's suggestion made me reconsider an incident that had occurred during the sea voyage with her mother. I had never really known what to make of it because of the vagueness of Helen's descriptions in her letters, but it appeared that Barbara had suffered some kind of psychological breakdown during the trip. "Bar has had a smash—emotional and nervous," Helen wrote to her friend Anne. "She has lost interest in things, in living, in writing. She says, herself, she is 'homesick.' But there's a reason. She has missed her father terribly." And then she added more ominously, "She is in a critical condition, and likely to do anything from running away to suicide."

The voyage hadn't been the idyllic mother-daughter adventure that Helen had portrayed in her books. Barbara had been "in bad shape for some months." While I didn't doubt that something serious had happened, I wondered if Helen had made the situation sound more desperate than it was because of whom she was writing to. Anne and her husband were in touch with Wilson, and Helen often urged them to pass messages along to him. Had Helen hoped she would tell Wilson, and that he would feel bad and maybe finally send some money? Or at the very least emerge from hiding and voice some interest in his daughter?

But it was not a simple case of homesickness. Helen wrote to Anne, "The details in which this obsession worked itself along are not pleasant, are quite awful, in fact. They must wait." Helen repeatedly told Anne that she needed to talk to her about what had happened but that she would have to tell her later.

Upon landing in California, Barbara was placed in the care of a psychiatrist, Dr. Schoultz. Her mother left her in Pasadena

242

with friends and then went to Honolulu alone. Then Barbara ran away, which resulted in her arrest at the San Francisco hotel. In 1994, over sixty years after the incident, the *Boston Globe* wrote that she had "tried to kill herself by jumping out of a window." I had always understood that incident as a foiled escape attempt; until I came across this article I had never seen it characterized as an attempted suicide. Considering the length of time between the incident and the article, and the fact that the article contained other factual errors (for example, that Barbara's parents had separated after the incident when they had really separated before), it seemed unreliable.

But still, it seemed worth investigating the relevant details. Even if she hadn't been attempting suicide, I wanted to understand the level of her desperation and recklessness. Had she tried to climb out of a twelve-story window to avoid capture, it would still suggest some mental instability.

First I contacted the Los Angeles police (the case was handled by the LAPD because Barbara had run away from Los Angeles) to see if they had any records, but they did not.

I didn't know which boardinghouse Barbara had stayed in, but one article mentioned that it was on O'Farrell Street in the Tenderloin. I reviewed the buildings on the street and found that they were all between four and six stories—perhaps a reasonable height at which to try hiding on a fire escape. Her mother, father, and friends, who wrote to each other about the incident, never characterized it as a suicide attempt. I decided to think of it as an indicator of instability, but not conclusive proof that Barbara had been suicidal.

I had never known how much weight to give Barbara's breakdown in her later vanishing. Adolescence is often enough to drive anyone a bit mad. But in light of the private investigator's reaction, I knew it was time to consider that possibility more seriously.

There were several ominous lines in Alice's letters after Barbara's disappearance that suggested suicide. Every time Helen brought up a possible lead, Alice dismissed it, saying that there was no point in looking. I recalled her writing, "The dark waters closed over her long ago," in an obvious attempt to end the conversation. Her reluctance to search for Barbara suggested that she believed that something tragic had happened. Alice had meant this as a metaphor, but what if, as with Anderson's case, water did have something to do with it? Earlier, Alice had described Barbara's last letter, writing, "You see in it she was definitely thinking of the future." But the fact that this had ever been in question was revealing. She went on, "I refuse to believe anyone with so rich and deep a vitality would have ended her own life."

I flipped back through my files to reread Barbara's last letter for traces of "thinking of the future," or despair, and discovered something startling. Alice had sent the letter to Helen after Barbara had disappeared. According to Alice, it had been written in "the last two or three days before she vanished," but the very last letter in the file at Columbia was from over a month before her disappearance. So the last letter, perhaps the last one Barbara had ever written, was not in the archives, which was noteworthy considering that Helen had donated almost every scrap related to anything Barbara had ever done. The archives were so obviously a mother's attempt to undo her daughter's disappearance by including all traces of her and preserving them for future generations. To withhold such a significant letter—her last known words—was strange. There had been talk of the future in it, yes, but according to Alice, it had also revealed that Barbara "was suddenly overtaken by despair." I wondered if Helen had seen something in the letter she hadn't liked and decided to withhold or destroy it.

There was one fact about Barbara's disappearance that had always suggested to me that she had run away. The story went that she took thirty dollars with her the night she left, which equates to about five hundred dollars today. It was not enough money to live on for long, but enough to hold her over until she found work, and she had always been able to find work.

But then a startling thought occurred to me. I went to my notes and pulled out a copy of the police reports. There was no mention of the thirty dollars in them—and it seemed an important detail to omit. The only place I had ever seen the thirty dollars mentioned was in *Barbara: The Unconscious Autobiography of a Child Genius,* the book by Harold McCurdy, the child psychologist who had analyzed Barbara's letters and childhood materials. McCurdy had worked on the book with Helen. Helen must have been the one to tell him about the thirty dollars—and she must have heard it from Nick. Who else would have told her? But its absence from the police files made me wonder if somehow this detail had been invented. Maybe it was an offhand guess Nick had made about how much she *could* have taken and Helen had misunderstood it or wanted to believe it. Or maybe Nick had reason to give Helen false hope—to tell her something to throw her off the trail—but then why not mislead the police as well? The only certainty was that one of the key pieces of evidence that Barbara had gone off to start a new life was in question.

I called Conor McCourt back. He wasn't buying the idea that Nick had killed her. Barbara desperately didn't want Nick to leave, but she wasn't threatening to prevent him. She wanted him to give her a month before making his decision. He *could* divorce her, and divorce, generally, is easier than murder, Conor said. Of course we both agreed that this didn't rule out a crime of passion.

Conor also wasn't buying the idea that Barbara had run away and never gotten back in touch with her family. Her relationship with her father had improved. She had her sister, her half sisters, a bunch of friends, and her mother. I had to agree. Though the characters in her fiction vanished without saying good-bye, I wasn't sure Barbara herself was capable of this. In the past, she had always come back.

"Were those last letters despairing?" Conor asked.

"No," I said. "They were anxious and desperate, but not despairing." I paused, trying to consider the difference between despair and desperation. "Actually, I don't know," I said. Alice *had* described that final letter as despairing.

I reconsidered one of Barbara's last letters: "I still think there is a chance that the outcome will be a happy one," she wrote. But then there was the line after that, the one I had always read straight through, "but I would have to think that anyway, in order to live; so you can draw any conclusions you like from that!" *In order to live.* I had always taken "live" to mean "cope." "You can draw any conclusions you like from that" now sounded more ominous.

"Were there any bridges near her house?" Conor asked.

There were lots. Longfellow Bridge. Harvard Bridge. The Bunker Hill Bridge. The Boston University Bridge. The John W. Weeks Bridge. The Mystic River Bridge. They were all less than five miles from her apartment. She could have walked there. Harvard Bridge was closest, only 1.4 miles.

"Why a bridge?" I asked.

"Men shoot themselves, women jump," Conor said.

"Why?"

"I don't know," he said. "Maybe they don't want to mess up their faces. What time of year was it?"

"December," I said.

"Bodies sink in December and aren't found until the spring— if they're ever found at all. By spring they aren't identifiable. Things were different then. We're better at finding and identifying bodies now."

I thought back to one of the letters Barbara had written to Alice saying she had not been able to sleep after Nick had told her about the affair. She took sleeping pills every night because "the nights I could never stand without some kind of help in achieving oblivion." Achieving oblivion. Yes, if things were bad enough, oblivion could be tantalizing; nothingness preferable to mourning the end of your marriage. The desire wouldn't have to last long, just long enough to stand on the edge of a bridge with the frigid, choppy water below you. You could let yourself fall.

How does one simultaneously kill oneself and dispose of one's body? Water was one solution. I began investigating each of the bridges. The Mystic River Bridge is a cantilever truss bridge that extends for two miles. At its highest point, it stands 115 feet above the water. But construction didn't begin until nearly ten years after Barbara disappeared. The Harvard Bridge, constructed in 1887, seemed too low to the water to be fatal, though I found a case of a woman killing herself there in 2011. The Bunker Hill Bridge had been built in 2003. The Boston University Bridge also seemed too close to the water for a suicide, but I found articles about bodies being found near there and people attempting suicide from the bridge, so I couldn't rule it out. The Longfellow Bridge had been constructed at the turn of the twentieth century and people had committed suicide from it. The John W. Weeks Bridge was constructed in 1927, but it was also too low.

This left the Longfellow Bridge, the Boston University Bridge, and the Harvard Bridge. I started with local newspaper searches, with the name of the bridge and anything about bodies of women around the time of Barbara's disappearance. No news items turned up.

I decided to go through local papers more generally, using keywords like "drowned," "unidentified woman," "Jane Doe," "Charles River, woman," "missing woman," "body found," and "woman harbor victim" for the year after Barbara's disappearance. It wouldn't have had to have been a bridge. It could have been a boat. Or something else I wasn't considering. I was looking for bodies now. And searching newspapers allowed me to explore the possibilities of both suicide and foul play.

There were so many false leads, so many women who could have been Barbara but were, on closer examination, clearly not. Three weeks after Barbara vanished, a murdered woman's body was found drowned in Boston Harbor. But she was identified by her brother. A couple of weeks after Barbara disappeared, another woman appeared at Back Bay station and asked police to help her figure out who she was. But the amnesia victim was later identified as a Mrs. Hazel Gray of Bulrush Farm. A month after Barbara disappeared, the Coast Guard received a distress call. A ship was sinking off the coast of Nantucket with 146 people on board. A half dozen ships searched the icy waters for hours but found nothing. In the newspapers, they called the ship "the ghost ship." It turned out to be a hoax. The hoax's perpetrator, Byron C. Brown, was unrepentant, telling the authorities he would do it again if he had the chance.

A few weeks after Barbara disappeared, a woman suffering from frostbite and exhaustion had appeared at a residence in Hampton, New Hampshire, late at night. Barbara had been born in New Hampshire and had loved going to Lake Sunapee. This could be her, I thought. The woman refused to explain to police why she had been out in the cold and wouldn't give her name or address. They observed that she was well dressed and articulate, clearly educated. Later, at the hospital, nurses overheard her say things that led them to believe she was from Boston.

But upon further reading, I discovered that the woman was middle aged, weighed 160 pounds, and had false teeth. Later I found an article that stated simply that the woman had been identified and returned to Boston, never revealing her name.

There was one case that gave me pause. On December 23, about two weeks after Barbara disappeared, a woman's body was found in a Boston hotel room. The coroner determined that she was in her late twenties and 125 pounds—Barbara's weight. She had been beaten to death with the sharp end of her own high-heel shoe. On the dead woman's left thigh was a large, brilliantly colored butterfly tattoo, and so the woman became known as the Butterfly Girl. At first I dismissed the possibility of Barbara having a tattoo because I had heard no mention of her having one, and I had never really considered her the tattoo type. But then I recalled the passage from *The Voyage of the Norman D.*, when Barbara's only regret from the voyage was not getting a tattoo.

She had also made a compendium of ornate drawings and descriptions of imaginary butterflies. And there was, of course, the end of *The House Without Windows,* when butterflies land on Eepersip's wrists and she vanishes forever. The butterflies set Eepersip free.

The police were able to rustle up a couple of people who had seen the woman around the hotel. They reported that the Butterfly Girl called herself June Blaine, but that this was not her real name. One of the men reported that she had been a talented musician—a detail that stuck out to me considering that Barbara was an excellent violinist. The story of the Butterfly Girl was reported widely. When the police went through her hotel room, they found a picture of her and circulated it in the papers, hoping that this, along with the butterfly tattoo detail, would help them identify her. But no one came forward. Eventually, they were able to find the murderer. At the same court where two years later Nick would file for divorce, Anthony Konetsky was sentenced to a mere six to ten years in jail. June Blaine's true identity was never discovered. She remained at the mortuary for a month and then was interred, according to one newspaper, in a "pauper's grave—alone and unmourned."[*]

I looked at the picture. The woman's face was almost entirely in shadow and the inky newspaper print wasn't helping. She seemed pretty, but her features were hard to make out—her mouth was obscured. It could be Barbara, I thought. This wasn't how I had pictured Barbara's end, though. The details—drinking and being bludgeoned with a shoe—were sordid. I scanned for

---

[*]See Terry McShane, "The Case of the Butterfly Girl," *St. Petersburg Times,* April 11, 1943.

more articles about the Butterfly Girl until I came across a line that I had somehow missed before. The man who had originally identified the Butterfly Girl as June Blaine said he had known her for two years and had seen her at the hotel often and that he had felt sorry for her because she had been a heavy drinker during that time. This didn't fit with Barbara's story. There was evidence of her drinking whiskey when her marriage was falling apart but no mention of heavy drinking prior to that. I closed the files.

In the weeks after Barbara disappeared, women were murdered, found beaten, died in house fires and car accidents, and drowned in the Boston area. But in one way or another, I was able to rule them out as not Barbara. When I expanded my search to include the rest of the country, targeting places Barbara had been—Seattle, California, New Hampshire, and Vermont—the list of possible Barbaras became impossibly long. The sheer number of women who drowned off the coast of California, caught in a riptide, or killed in a boating accident, was staggering. There were so many women. Women in distress. Unclaimed women. Lost women. Unnamed women. Women in hiding. Deliberately hurt or killed—all by now forgotten.

TWENTY-FIVE

Around Christmas, P.J. and I decided to move to Mexico City. P.J. was still writing research reports for an education nonprofit, and most of this work could be done remotely. A girl we knew there had an airy apartment that we could rent for cheap. We could both do more writing if we were released from the financial grip of New York. P.J. was eager to spend time in Latin America and perfect his Spanish. I had spent almost no time in the region and wanted to see it. But I also wanted to make a gesture to P.J. that said: Where you go, I go.

But we were leaving great friends. We had created a tribe in New York, perhaps more so than any place we had ever lived. These were the people who had seen me through a painful period in my marriage. But more simply, I had fun with them. A few nights before we planned to leave, my grad school professor threw a beautiful farewell dinner with a few grad school friends and another mentor. She cooked shrimp, we drank wine, and she toasted us, saying that we were like family—a comment that moved me because I felt that she meant it. As I looked around the table, I realized we were leaving New York before the party was over. The house was still filled with people. There was chatter in every room. Something dazzling could still happen, and I might miss it. I was leaving while I was still loved. If I stayed another year, would they grow sick of me? I felt a small ripping sensation, like a fruit torn too early from a tree. But I still believe it is better to go early than to see the party disband with nothing but dirty plates left behind.

The scene at the airport was different from the one three years earlier, when we had left for Southeast Asia. We had our backpacks, but also a suitcase each. All the rest of our belongings were sold or placed on our stoop and somehow reabsorbed by Brooklyn. There was no large good-bye party at the airport. Just my parents drove us. We had said good-bye to P.J.'s family the night before. My parents parked at the departure gate curb, got out of the car, and hugged us. "A picture," my mom said. "Let me take a picture." I think she wanted our leaving to be remarkable, but we all knew it wasn't anymore. Inside the airport, we faced the agent.

"Your return tickets?" she said.

"We don't have them," P.J. said.

"Then you can't get on the plane."

On our laptops at a table near the JetBlue counter, we bought tickets to attend a wedding in California in the summer, just sliding in under Mexico's six-month tourist visa time limit. We showed the woman the tickets on our phones and she printed our boarding passes.

"Have a nice trip to Mexico," she said.

On the plane, I became drowsy and woke just before landing. It was night. There were dark mountains below, and it looked like someone had thrown silver and gold jewels that had gathered shimmering all around their bases. This was the city at night, a metropolis, one of the largest in the world—certainly the largest I had ever been to.

In Mexico, P.J. moved me again. I spoke very little Spanish, so his fluency, his ease maneuvering through a city he had never been to, seemed miraculous to me. A few months later I watched him interview a woman whose son had been kidnapped and probably killed by the cartels in Guerrero state. I could catch only bits and phrases of what they were saying, but I admired P.J.'s manner, both professional and compassionate. He sat on the curb in front of a government building where a group of parents had chained themselves to a fence in protest, his legs long and thin like a grasshopper's as he sat beside the woman, nodding and occasionally asking questions softly. I could tell she was comforted by his presence. I was comforted by his presence.

We loved almost everything about Mexico. The *camote* sales-man who walked around our neighborhood with a little coal oven that whistled. The colorful rows of colonial-era houses with their high ceilings. Parque México was like walking into the American Kennel Club. I saw breeds of dog that I had only ever seen on television: Afghan hounds, hairless Chinese crested dogs, the komondor, which was all hair, its perfectly groomed mane com-pletely covering its eyes and reaching all the way to the floor. We ate *huaraches* elbow to elbow at the crowded market. We bought Oaxacan cheese from the same friendly, middle-aged woman every week. We began to call her *our* cheese woman and were baffled when one week she wasn't there. On the weekends, in the narrow courtyard beside our building, we played soccer with the kids who lived in the apartment below us. We used an old lady's station wagon as one of the goals. We never held back even though we were twice their size, and still we often lost.

I started kickboxing classes in a small gym above a rowdy bar. No one in the gym spoke English except a couple of the girls in the class. The man who owned the gym was a boy-faced mixed martial arts fighter who would sometimes sleep on the floor during our class. Our instructor would shout things at us in Spanish, and over time I came to understand what he was saying. *¡Más rápido! ¡Rodillas más altas! ¡Más fuerte!* Faster! Knees higher! Stronger!

We visited a friend who was studying textile design in a small town outside of Oaxaca City. We saw a wedding replete with a marching band and a parade. People hoisted enormous papier-mâché puppets of the bride and groom in the air. We walked down the narrow winding streets with old brick walls and simple white plaster houses with terra-cotta roofs. I liked the aesthetic of the place: spare with occasional bursts of color. All around us, jacaranda trees were in bloom. We walked through a field, be-friending a large, happy dog who eventually abandoned us for more exciting things. As the sun set, we stopped at a little outdoor restaurant that served only *mole* and overlooked a field where puppies were frolicking. I could imagine staying in Mexico for a long time. I could see an old truck, a ranch-style house, and dogs. I wondered how long this feeling would last.

After four months in Mexico, P.J. got a case of what is known as Montezuma's revenge. He got out of bed only to projectile vomit in the direction of our toilet. I wasn't worried; Montezuma had already gotten his revenge on me, and I knew it wouldn't last. I brought Gatorade and plain crackers to his bedside. Occasionally,

I poked my head in and watched him while he slept; his face, even in sleep, was worried and worn out.

I felt a fierce protectiveness over him. I saw now that our marriage wasn't really about vows. I wasn't there because I had said I would be, but because I wanted to be. And if I had weathered months when I hadn't really wanted to be there, when I had preferred the comforts of others, I still anticipated wanting to come back to him. Even at our coldest, most unfeeling moments, I continued to admire him—and admiration seemed the life-blood of our marriage now. It was possible that one day, one or both of us wouldn't want to stay anymore. It was possible that our store of admiration would become exhausted, the lifeblood of our marriage drained. And if that were the case, one or both of us would leave.

Oddly, this comforted me. If there were vows, they were vows to wait, to make sure that there wasn't something worthy still there between us to be unearthed. I didn't want P.J. to stay if he didn't want to just because he had said he would. I didn't want to have to stay if I didn't want to. The comfort was in my own feelings of strength, that I could withstand his departure, that I would have the inner power to know when something was over and to let it be.

But maybe that is just a thought you can have when your relationship feels strong, when you feel strong, and if the moment really presented itself, you might cling to a person who doesn't want you anymore because you are desperate, because you need someone and will accept any shred of connection, no matter how paltry, because it is preferable to the dull ache of loneliness and abandonment.

I was still young, in that sweet spot where I looked forward to the parts of life that were ahead of me, but felt a little more confident about my place in the world. I knew that old age, middle age, or even just the next day held things I didn't understand. It occurred to me that P.J. and I were circling around each other, that this was just the first cycle in our marriage. I didn't really agree with Michael's analysis that Barbara's story was about running away and mine was about coming home. Both were about perpetual motion. We move toward one another and we move away. We draw near, we retreat. We start over again. Perhaps the chase has only just begun.

That night P.J. held my hand while he slept. I didn't mind the clammy feverishness of his palm. I let his hand linger in mine a little longer, until he rolled over, dreaming.

I still talked to Michael, but less. The interactions were usually warm and wistful. A few months after I went to Mexico, he met a woman. I could tell it was serious. Their only real problem seemed to be that she was allergic to his cats. Perhaps my leaving was the sign he needed to move on. Perhaps he would have moved on anyway. I thought about Michael in his space capsule, passing by my blue planet. I felt him drifting out of my orbit, heading toward new planets, new lives. My pull had faded for him and I felt pulled by P.J. again. Michael used to joke that when I died, he would weep at my funeral, prompting my relatives to nudge each other and ask, "Who is that old crying guy?" But he smoked, so I figured I would live longer and go to his funeral and alarm his relatives. I told Michael this, and he said that there was nothing more glamorous than having a mystery woman crying at your funeral. Our relationship was unblemished by a life lived together.

But I see the value in both: the elegance of the unopened door and the raw beauty of shared experience. Michael and I would be in touch. Or maybe we wouldn't. There was no way to know.

One afternoon, P.J. and I walked down a large, tree-lined thoroughfare in Roma Norte. People sat in sidewalk cafés eating lunch, or bought or sold things, or just strolled. At a distance behind us, we heard sirens blaring. Four police cars processed slowly down the street. None of the cars ahead of them moved to get out of their way. People crossed unhurried. I wondered why, if there was an emergency, they were driving so slowly, making no effort to move forward in traffic. It was then that I noticed the small flyers taped to their windows. I had to plug my ears from the sirens to get close enough to see: on the page, there was a photograph of a smiling, pretty young girl, perhaps in her early twenties. She was missing. The girl was wearing a cap and gown. I imagined that her family had deliberately chosen the cap and gown picture because they wanted to evoke the idea that she was a person with hopes, a person who wanted things, a person who had made plans.

Wanting, having plans, believing that you will live and possibly live well suddenly seemed such a vulnerable notion. We are guaranteed none of it. The barrier between fortune and ruin, life and death is unnervingly small. I was chilled by the scene: the piercing sound of the sirens, the police cars' funereal procession, the hopelessly small poster. It conveyed both a sense of emergency—A girl has disappeared right from our midst! Did you notice?—and the sense that we could do nothing about it. Her story was already over.

It occurred to me, as it often does in moments like those, that perhaps it was time to move on—from Barbara, from the questions that had haunted me about the contradictions of marriage and the story of this one woman's life. There were other things to be concerned with, other people and things to learn about, other causes to invest myself in. But even as I told myself this, with the police procession still in view, I was struck by another thought. I still just want to know.

ACKNOWLEDGMENTS

I am grateful to the faculty and students at the New York University Arthur L. Carter Journalism Institute, especially those from the Literary Reportage and Cultural Reporting and Criticism programs. Thanks to the Banff Centre for Arts and Creativity, especially the editors in the Literary Journalism program, Charlotte Gill, Ian Brown, and Victor Dwyer, and the 2015 residency cohort. Many thanks to Katie Roiphe, my mentor, and to my agent, Flip Brophy, and my editor, Joy de Menil, for your commitment to this project. For research help, many thanks to Paul Collins, Marissa Bourgain, Conor McCourt, the Columbia University Rare Book & Manuscript Library staff, and especially to Stefan Cooke, Barbara's nephew and most dedicated biographer. To my friends and early draft readers, Anneke Rautenbach, Maddie Gressel, Robert Downey, and Michael Lista. Many thanks to Gabby and Tata. Many, many thanks to Mom, Dad, and Jenny. And to P.J.